50 Taste of Mexico Recipes for Home

By: Kelly Johnson

Table of Contents

- Tacos al Pastor
- Guacamole
- Enchiladas Verdes
- Pozole
- Chiles Rellenos
- Sopa de Tortilla (Tortilla Soup)
- Carnitas
- Mole Poblano
- Tamales
- Ceviche
- Quesadillas
- Arroz con Pollo (Chicken with Rice)
- Fajitas
- Chile con Carne
- Tostadas
- Pico de Gallo
- Birria
- Flan
- Churros
- Empanadas
- Aguachile
- Camarones a la Diabla (Spicy Shrimp)
- Cochinita Pibil
- Elote (Mexican Street Corn)
- Huevos Rancheros
- Tlayudas
- Molletes
- Papas con Chorizo (Potatoes with Chorizo)
- Sopes
- Champurrado (Mexican Hot Chocolate)
- Pan de Elote (Cornbread)
- Tacos de Pescado (Fish Tacos)
- Barbacoa
- Horchata
- Tamale Pie
- Tostadas de Tinga

- Caldo de Res (Beef Soup)
- Jicama Salad
- Alambre
- Gorditas
- Cochinita Pibil
- Birria de Res
- Chiles en Nogada
- Mexican Rice
- Polvorones (Mexican Wedding Cookies)
- Camotes Enmielados (Candied Sweet Potatoes)
- Tacos de Canasta
- Sopa Azteca
- Nopalitos Salad (Cactus Salad)
- Rosca de Reyes

Tacos al Pastor

Ingredients:

- **Marinade:**
    - Achiote paste
    - Guajillo chilies
    - Garlic
    - Pineapple juice
    - Orange juice
    - Vinegar
    - Cumin
    - Oregano
    - Salt and pepper
- **Pork:**
    - Pork shoulder or pork butt, thinly sliced
- **Toppings:**
    - Pineapple, thinly sliced
    - Onion, finely chopped
    - Cilantro, chopped
    - Lime wedges
    - Salsa verde or salsa roja
    - Corn tortillas

Instructions:

1. **Prepare the Marinade:**
    - Blend achiote paste, guajillo chilies (soaked and deseeded), garlic, pineapple juice, orange juice, vinegar, cumin, oregano, salt, and pepper until smooth.
2. **Marinate the Pork:**
    - Coat thinly sliced pork shoulder or pork butt with the marinade. Let it marinate in the refrigerator for at least 2 hours, preferably overnight.
3. **Cooking the Meat:**
    - Traditionally, tacos al pastor are cooked on a vertical spit (trompo), but you can also use a grill or oven. If using a spit, stack the marinated pork slices on the spit and cook until charred and cooked through.
4. **Assembling Tacos:**
    - Once cooked, thinly slice the meat from the spit. Serve on warm corn tortillas topped with pineapple, chopped onions, cilantro, and salsa. Squeeze fresh lime juice over the tacos before serving.
5. **Enjoy:**
    - Tacos al Pastor are typically served with additional salsa on the side and are delicious enjoyed immediately.

This dish combines savory and spicy flavors with a hint of sweetness from the pineapple, making it a favorite among taco enthusiasts worldwide.

Guacamole

Ingredients:

- 3 ripe avocados
- 1 lime, juiced
- 1/2 teaspoon salt, or to taste
- 1/2 teaspoon ground cumin
- 1/2 teaspoon cayenne pepper (optional, for heat)
- 1/2 medium red onion, finely diced
- 2 roma tomatoes, seeded and diced
- 1/4 cup fresh cilantro, chopped
- 1-2 cloves garlic, minced

Instructions:

1. **Prepare the Avocados:**
   - Cut the avocados in half and remove the pits. Scoop the flesh into a mixing bowl.
2. **Mash the Avocados:**
   - Use a fork or potato masher to mash the avocados to your desired consistency (some like it chunky, some like it smooth).
3. **Add Lime Juice and Seasonings:**
   - Squeeze the lime juice over the mashed avocados. Add salt, ground cumin, and cayenne pepper (if using). Mix well to combine.
4. **Add Remaining Ingredients:**
   - Fold in the diced red onion, diced tomatoes, chopped cilantro, and minced garlic. Mix gently until everything is evenly distributed.
5. **Adjust Seasonings:**
   - Taste the guacamole and adjust salt, lime juice, or other seasonings to your preference.
6. **Serve:**
   - Transfer the guacamole to a serving bowl. You can garnish with additional cilantro or a sprinkle of cayenne pepper. Serve immediately with tortilla chips or as a topping for tacos, burritos, or other Mexican dishes.
7. **Storage:**
   - If you have leftovers, store the guacamole in an airtight container in the refrigerator. Press plastic wrap directly onto the surface of the guacamole to prevent browning. It's best consumed within a day or two.

Enjoy your homemade guacamole as a delicious snack or accompaniment to your favorite Mexican meals!

Enchiladas Verdes

Ingredients:

For the Enchilada Sauce:

- 1 lb (about 500g) tomatillos, husked and rinsed
- 2-3 jalapeño or serrano peppers (adjust to taste)
- 1 small onion, peeled and quartered
- 2 cloves garlic, peeled
- 1 cup chicken broth (or vegetable broth for vegetarian option)
- 1/2 cup chopped cilantro
- Salt to taste
- 1 tablespoon vegetable oil

For the Enchiladas:

- 12-14 corn tortillas
- 2 cups shredded cooked chicken (or cheese for vegetarian option)
- 1/2 cup crumbled queso fresco (optional, for garnish)
- Chopped cilantro, for garnish
- Sour cream or Mexican crema, for serving (optional)

Instructions:

1. Prepare the Enchilada Sauce:

1. **Roast the Vegetables:**
   - Preheat the broiler in your oven. Place tomatillos, jalapeños (or serranos), onion, and garlic on a baking sheet. Broil for about 5-7 minutes until they are charred and softened, turning halfway through.
2. **Blend the Sauce:**
   - Transfer the roasted vegetables along with any juices from the baking sheet into a blender. Add chicken broth, cilantro, and salt. Blend until smooth.
3. **Cook the Sauce:**
   - Heat oil in a saucepan over medium heat. Pour in the blended sauce and bring to a simmer. Cook for about 10 minutes, stirring occasionally, until the sauce thickens slightly. Taste and adjust seasoning if needed. Remove from heat.

2. Prepare the Enchiladas:

1. **Prepare the Tortillas:**
   - In a separate skillet, heat a small amount of oil over medium-high heat. Lightly fry each corn tortilla for about 5-10 seconds per side until softened. Drain on paper towels.

2. **Assemble the Enchiladas:**
   - Preheat your oven to 350°F (175°C). Take each tortilla and dip it into the warm enchilada sauce to coat both sides. Place some shredded chicken (or cheese for vegetarian option) in the center of each tortilla and roll it up. Place seam-side down in a baking dish.
3. **Top with Sauce and Cheese:**
   - Pour the remaining enchilada sauce over the rolled tortillas, covering them evenly. Sprinkle with crumbled queso fresco if using.
4. **Bake:**
   - Cover the baking dish with foil and bake in the preheated oven for about 20 minutes, or until the enchiladas are heated through and the sauce is bubbly.
5. **Serve:**
   - Remove from the oven and garnish with chopped cilantro. Serve hot, accompanied by sour cream or Mexican crema if desired.

Enjoy these delicious Enchiladas Verdes as a main dish, served with rice and beans for a complete Mexican meal!

Pozole

Ingredients:

For the Pozole:

- 1 pound (450g) pork shoulder or pork butt, cut into chunks
- 1 onion, chopped
- 4 cloves garlic, minced
- 2 cups canned hominy, drained and rinsed
- 6 cups chicken broth
- 2 dried ancho chilies, stems and seeds removed
- 1 dried guajillo chili, stem and seeds removed
- 1 teaspoon dried oregano
- 1 teaspoon ground cumin
- Salt and pepper to taste

For serving (optional):

- Shredded lettuce or cabbage
- Sliced radishes
- Chopped cilantro
- Diced onion
- Lime wedges
- Avocado slices
- Mexican crema or sour cream
- Tortilla chips or tostadas

Instructions:

1. **Prepare the Chilies:**
   - Bring a small pot of water to a boil. Add the dried ancho and guajillo chilies, then remove from heat and let them soak for about 15-20 minutes until softened. Once softened, drain the chilies.
2. **Make the Pozole:**
   - In a large pot or Dutch oven, heat some oil over medium-high heat. Add the chopped onion and minced garlic, sautéing until softened and fragrant, about 3-4 minutes.
   - Add the pork pieces to the pot and brown them on all sides, about 5-7 minutes.
   - While the pork is browning, place the softened chilies in a blender along with 1 cup of chicken broth. Blend until smooth to make a chili paste.
   - Once the pork is browned, add the hominy, remaining chicken broth, oregano, ground cumin, and the chili paste to the pot. Stir well to combine.
   - Bring the mixture to a boil, then reduce the heat to low. Cover and simmer for about 1.5 to 2 hours, or until the pork is tender and the flavors have melded

together. Stir occasionally and add more broth if needed to achieve your desired consistency.
      - Season with salt and pepper to taste.
   3. **Serve:**
      - Ladle the pozole into bowls. Serve hot with shredded lettuce or cabbage, sliced radishes, chopped cilantro, diced onion, lime wedges, avocado slices, Mexican crema or sour cream, and tortilla chips or tostadas on the side.

Enjoy your homemade Pozole Rojo! Adjust the spice level to your preference by adding more or less chili paste. It's a comforting and flavorful dish perfect for sharing with family and friends.

Chiles Rellenos

Ingredients:

For the Chiles Rellenos:

- 4 large poblano peppers
- 1 cup shredded cheese (like Oaxaca cheese, Monterey Jack, or queso fresco)
- 1 cup cooked shredded chicken or pork (optional)
- 1/2 cup all-purpose flour
- 4 large eggs, separated
- Salt and pepper to taste
- Oil for frying

For the Tomato Sauce (Salsa de Jitomate):

- 4 large tomatoes, chopped
- 1/2 onion, chopped
- 2 cloves garlic, minced
- 1 tablespoon vegetable oil
- 1/2 teaspoon dried oregano
- Salt and pepper to taste

Instructions:

1. **Prepare the Poblano Peppers:**
    - Roast the poblano peppers over an open flame or under the broiler until the skin is charred and blistered. Place them in a bowl, cover with plastic wrap or a kitchen towel, and let them sweat for about 10-15 minutes. This will make it easier to peel off the skin.
    - Peel off the charred skin from the poblano peppers. Make a slit lengthwise on one side of each pepper and carefully remove the seeds and membranes, creating a pocket for the filling.
2. **Make the Filling:**
    - In a bowl, mix together the shredded cheese and cooked shredded chicken or pork, if using. Season with salt and pepper to taste.
    - Stuff each poblano pepper with the filling, being careful not to overfill them so they can still be closed.
3. **Prepare the Batter:**
    - Separate the egg yolks from the whites into two separate bowls.
    - In a bowl with the egg yolks, add the flour and a pinch of salt. Mix until smooth.
    - In the bowl with the egg whites, beat them until stiff peaks form.
    - Gently fold the beaten egg whites into the yolk and flour mixture until well combined. This creates a light and airy batter.
4. **Fry the Chiles Rellenos:**

- In a large skillet, heat enough oil over medium-high heat for frying (about 1 inch deep).
- Dip each stuffed poblano pepper into the batter, making sure it is well coated.
- Carefully place the battered pepper into the hot oil and fry until golden brown on all sides, turning as needed. This should take about 4-5 minutes per side.
- Remove the fried chile relleno from the oil and place on a plate lined with paper towels to drain excess oil. Repeat with the remaining peppers.

5. **Make the Tomato Sauce:**
    - In a blender, combine the chopped tomatoes, onion, and garlic. Blend until smooth.
    - In a saucepan, heat the vegetable oil over medium heat. Pour in the blended tomato mixture and add the dried oregano, salt, and pepper.
    - Simmer the sauce for about 10-15 minutes, stirring occasionally, until it thickens slightly and the flavors meld together.

6. **Serve:**
    - Serve the Chiles Rellenos hot, drizzled with the tomato sauce on top. They can be accompanied by Mexican rice, refried beans, and a side of warm tortillas.

Enjoy your homemade Chiles Rellenos with their crispy exterior and savory filling! It's a wonderful dish that showcases the flavors and textures of traditional Mexican cuisine.

Sopa de Tortilla (Tortilla Soup)

Ingredients:

For the Soup:

- 2 tablespoons vegetable oil
- 1 onion, chopped
- 3 cloves garlic, minced
- 1 jalapeño or serrano pepper, seeded and finely chopped (optional, for heat)
- 1 can (14.5 oz) diced tomatoes
- 1 teaspoon ground cumin
- 1 teaspoon chili powder
- 6 cups chicken or vegetable broth
- Salt and pepper to taste
- 1 cup cooked shredded chicken (optional)
- 2 cups tortilla chips, lightly crushed or broken into pieces
- Juice of 1 lime

For Garnish:

- Tortilla strips or tortilla chips (for topping)
- Avocado slices
- Fresh cilantro, chopped
- Mexican crema or sour cream
- Shredded cheese (like Monterey Jack or cheddar)
- Lime wedges

Instructions:

1. **Prepare the Soup Base:**
    - Heat the vegetable oil in a large pot over medium heat. Add the chopped onion and cook until softened, about 5 minutes.
    - Add the minced garlic and chopped jalapeño or serrano pepper (if using), and cook for another 2 minutes until fragrant.
2. **Add Tomatoes and Spices:**
    - Stir in the diced tomatoes with their juices, ground cumin, and chili powder. Cook for about 5 minutes, stirring occasionally.
3. **Simmer the Soup:**
    - Pour in the chicken or vegetable broth and bring the mixture to a boil. Reduce the heat to low and let it simmer for 15-20 minutes to allow the flavors to meld together.
    - Season with salt and pepper to taste.
4. **Blend the Soup (optional):**

- For a smoother texture, you can use an immersion blender to blend part of the soup until smooth. Alternatively, leave it chunky if you prefer.
5. **Add Chicken and Tortilla Chips:**
    - If using shredded chicken, add it to the soup and simmer for another 5 minutes until heated through.
    - Stir in the crushed tortilla chips and let them soften in the soup for a couple of minutes.
6. **Finish with Lime Juice:**
    - Squeeze in the juice of one lime to brighten up the flavors of the soup. Adjust the seasoning if needed.
7. **Serve:**
    - Ladle the Sopa de Tortilla into bowls. Top each serving with tortilla strips or chips, avocado slices, chopped cilantro, a dollop of Mexican crema or sour cream, shredded cheese, and a lime wedge on the side.

Enjoy your homemade Sopa de Tortilla! It's a perfect dish for any time of year, warming and full of vibrant flavors. Adjust the toppings and spiciness to your liking for a personalized touch.

Carnitas

Ingredients:

- 3-4 lbs (1.5-2 kg) pork shoulder or pork butt, cut into large chunks
- 1 onion, quartered
- 4 cloves garlic, smashed
- 1 orange, juiced (about 1/2 cup)
- 1 lime, juiced
- 1/2 cup water or chicken broth
- 2 bay leaves
- 1 teaspoon dried oregano
- 1 teaspoon ground cumin
- 1 teaspoon ground coriander
- 1 teaspoon chili powder (optional, for spice)
- Salt and pepper to taste
- 2 tablespoons vegetable oil, for searing

Instructions:

1. **Preheat the Oven:**
   - Preheat your oven to 325°F (160°C).
2. **Prepare the Pork:**
   - Season the pork chunks generously with salt and pepper.
3. **Sear the Pork:**
   - Heat vegetable oil in a large oven-safe pot or Dutch oven over medium-high heat.
   - Working in batches, sear the pork pieces on all sides until browned and caramelized. This step helps develop flavor. Remove and set aside.
4. **Braise the Pork:**
   - In the same pot, add the quartered onion and smashed garlic. Sauté for a few minutes until fragrant.
   - Return the seared pork to the pot. Add the bay leaves, dried oregano, ground cumin, ground coriander, and chili powder (if using).
   - Pour in the orange juice, lime juice, and water or chicken broth. The liquid should come up about halfway up the sides of the pork pieces.
5. **Cook in the Oven:**
   - Cover the pot with a lid and transfer it to the preheated oven.
   - Braise the pork in the oven for about 2.5 to 3 hours, or until the meat is very tender and easily shreds with a fork.
6. **Shred the Pork:**
   - Once the pork is cooked and tender, remove it from the oven.
   - Using two forks, shred the pork into smaller pieces. You can discard any large pieces of fat or connective tissue.
7. **Crisp the Carnitas (Optional):**

- For crispy carnitas, heat a large skillet over medium-high heat.
- Add a bit of vegetable oil and spread the shredded pork in an even layer in the skillet. Let it cook without stirring for a few minutes to develop a crispy crust on the bottom.
- Stir and continue to cook until the carnitas are crispy and golden brown in spots. Remove from heat.

8. **Serve:**
    - Serve the carnitas hot as a filling for tacos, burritos, or as a main dish with rice and beans.
    - Garnish with fresh cilantro, diced onions, salsa, avocado slices, lime wedges, or any other toppings of your choice.

Enjoy your homemade carnitas! The slow braising process ensures tender, flavorful pork that's perfect for any Mexican-inspired meal. Adjust seasonings and spices to suit your taste preferences.

Mole Poblano

Ingredients:

For the Mole Sauce:

- 3 dried ancho chilies
- 3 dried pasilla chilies
- 3 dried mulato chilies
- 2 tablespoons vegetable oil
- 1 onion, chopped
- 4 cloves garlic, minced
- 1/2 cup almonds
- 1/2 cup raisins
- 1/4 cup sesame seeds
- 1/4 cup pumpkin seeds (pepitas)
- 1/2 teaspoon ground cinnamon
- 1/2 teaspoon ground cloves
- 1/2 teaspoon ground coriander
- 1/2 teaspoon ground cumin
- 1/2 teaspoon dried oregano
- 1/4 teaspoon ground black pepper
- 3 cups chicken broth
- 1 tablet Mexican chocolate (such as Ibarra or Abuelita), chopped (about 3 ounces)
- Salt to taste
- Sugar (optional, to taste)

For the Mole Poblano:

- 1 whole chicken (about 3-4 lbs), cut into parts, or turkey pieces
- Salt and pepper to taste
- Vegetable oil for frying

For Serving:

- Cooked white rice
- Sesame seeds (for garnish)
- Warm corn tortillas

Instructions:

1. **Prepare the Chilies:**
    - Remove the stems and seeds from the dried ancho, pasilla, and mulato chilies. Heat a dry skillet over medium heat and toast the chilies for about 1-2 minutes per side, until fragrant. Place them in a bowl and cover with hot water. Let them soak for about 20-30 minutes until softened.
2. **Prepare the Mole Sauce:**

- In a large saucepan or Dutch oven, heat the vegetable oil over medium heat. Add the chopped onion and minced garlic, sautéing until softened and translucent, about 5 minutes.
- Add the almonds, raisins, sesame seeds, and pumpkin seeds to the pan. Cook for another 3-4 minutes, stirring constantly, until the nuts and seeds are lightly toasted.
- Stir in the ground cinnamon, cloves, coriander, cumin, oregano, and black pepper. Cook for another minute until fragrant.
- Drain the soaked chilies and add them to the pan along with 3 cups of chicken broth. Bring to a simmer and cook for about 10 minutes, allowing the flavors to meld together.
- Transfer the mixture to a blender and blend until smooth. You may need to do this in batches. Be careful when blending hot liquids.
- Pour the blended sauce back into the saucepan. Add the chopped Mexican chocolate and stir until it melts and incorporates into the sauce. Season with salt to taste. If the sauce is too bitter, you can add a bit of sugar to balance the flavors.

3. **Cook the Chicken or Turkey:**
    - Season the chicken or turkey pieces with salt and pepper.
    - In a large skillet, heat a tablespoon of vegetable oil over medium-high heat. Brown the chicken or turkey pieces on all sides until golden brown, working in batches if necessary.
    - Once browned, transfer the chicken or turkey pieces to the simmering mole sauce.

4. **Simmer the Mole:**
    - Cover the saucepan and let the chicken or turkey simmer in the mole sauce over low heat for about 1 to 1.5 hours, until the meat is tender and fully cooked. Stir occasionally to prevent sticking.

5. **Serve:**
    - Serve the Mole Poblano hot over cooked white rice.
    - Garnish with sesame seeds and serve with warm corn tortillas on the side.

Enjoy your homemade Mole Poblano! It's a labor-intensive dish but well worth the effort for its rich and delicious flavors that are emblematic of Mexican cuisine.

Tamales

Ingredients:

For the masa:

- 2 cups masa harina (corn masa flour)
- 1 teaspoon baking powder
- 1/2 teaspoon salt
- 1 1/3 cups chicken broth (or water)
- 2/3 cup lard or vegetable shortening

For the filling:

- 1 pound pork shoulder or pork butt, cut into small chunks
- 1 onion, chopped
- 2 cloves garlic, minced
- 1 teaspoon cumin powder
- 1 teaspoon chili powder (adjust to taste)
- Salt and pepper to taste
- 1 tablespoon vegetable oil
- 1/2 cup chicken broth

For assembling:

- Dried corn husks, soaked in warm water for 1-2 hours to soften

Instructions:

1. Prepare the pork filling:

- In a large skillet or frying pan, heat the vegetable oil over medium-high heat.
- Add the chopped onion and cook until translucent, about 3-4 minutes.
- Add the minced garlic and cook for another 1-2 minutes until fragrant.
- Add the pork chunks to the skillet and brown them on all sides.
- Season with cumin powder, chili powder, salt, and pepper.
- Pour in 1/2 cup of chicken broth, reduce heat to low, cover, and simmer for 1 to 1.5 hours until the pork is tender and cooked through. Check occasionally and add more broth if needed to keep it from drying out. Once done, shred the pork with forks.

2. Prepare the masa dough:

- In a large mixing bowl, combine the masa harina, baking powder, and salt.
- In a separate bowl, beat the lard or vegetable shortening until fluffy.
- Gradually add the masa harina mixture to the lard, alternating with chicken broth, and mix until a dough forms. The consistency should be like soft cookie dough. You may need more or less broth depending on the humidity and the brand of masa harina.

3. Assemble the tamales:

- Drain the corn husks and pat them dry with paper towels.
- Take a softened corn husk and spread about 2 tablespoons of masa dough onto the center, leaving space around the edges.
- Spoon a tablespoon or so of the pork filling down the center of the masa.
- Fold one side of the corn husk over the filling, then fold the other side over to cover. Fold up the bottom end of the husk.
- Place the tamale seam-side down on a tray and repeat with the remaining masa and filling.

4. Steam the tamales:

- Arrange the tamales vertically in a steamer pot with the open end facing up. If you don't have a steamer, you can use a large pot with a steamer basket.
- Add water to the bottom of the pot (below the steamer basket), cover with a lid, and steam over medium heat for about 1 to 1.5 hours. Check occasionally and add more water to the pot as needed.
- The tamales are done when the masa easily pulls away from the husks. Let them rest for a few minutes before serving.

5. Serve and enjoy:

- Unwrap the tamales from the corn husks before serving. They can be enjoyed plain or with salsa, guacamole, or other toppings of your choice.

This recipe makes approximately 12-16 tamales, depending on the size. Adjust seasoning and filling ingredients according to your preferences. Tamales can also be made with other fillings such as chicken, beef, cheese, or vegetables, so feel free to experiment!

Ceviche

Ingredients:

- 1 pound firm white fish fillets (such as sea bass, snapper, or tilapia), cut into small cubes
- 1 cup freshly squeezed lime juice (about 8-10 limes)
- 1 red onion, thinly sliced
- 1-2 tomatoes, diced
- 1-2 jalapeño peppers, seeded and finely chopped (optional, for heat)
- 1/2 cup chopped cilantro leaves
- Salt and pepper to taste
- 1-2 tablespoons olive oil (optional)
- Additional lime wedges for serving
- Tortilla chips or crackers for serving

Instructions:

1. Prepare the fish:

- Cut the fish fillets into small, bite-sized cubes and place them in a shallow dish or bowl.

2. Marinate the fish:

- Pour the freshly squeezed lime juice over the fish, making sure it's fully submerged. The acid in the lime juice will "cook" the fish. Cover the dish with plastic wrap and refrigerate for about 15-20 minutes. The fish should turn opaque and firm when it's ready.

3. Prepare the vegetables:

- While the fish is marinating, thinly slice the red onion, dice the tomatoes, and finely chop the jalapeño peppers (if using). Chop the cilantro leaves as well.

4. Combine the ceviche:

- Drain most of the lime juice from the fish (leaving a little is fine for flavor). Add the sliced red onion, diced tomatoes, chopped jalapeños (if using), and chopped cilantro to the fish.
- Season with salt and pepper to taste. If desired, drizzle with olive oil for added richness.

5. Mix gently:

- Gently toss everything together until well combined. Be careful not to break up the fish cubes too much.

6. Chill and serve:

- Cover the ceviche and refrigerate for at least 30 minutes to allow the flavors to meld together.
- Serve the ceviche chilled, garnished with additional cilantro leaves and lime wedges. Enjoy with tortilla chips or crackers.

Tips:

- **Fish selection:** Use fresh, high-quality fish that is suitable for raw consumption.
- **Citrus juice:** Freshly squeezed lime juice is traditional, but you can also use a combination of lime and lemon juice.
- **Adjust seasoning:** Taste the ceviche before serving and adjust the seasoning as needed with more salt, pepper, or lime juice.
- **Variations:** Ceviche can be made with shrimp, scallops, squid, or a combination of seafood. You can also add diced avocado, cucumber, or mango for additional flavor and texture.

Ceviche is best enjoyed fresh, shortly after preparing. It's perfect for warm weather gatherings or as a light and flavorful appetizer.

Quesadillas

Ingredients:

- 4 large flour tortillas

- 2 cups shredded cheese (such as cheddar, Monterey Jack, or a Mexican cheese blend)
- Optional fillings: cooked chicken, beef, beans, sautéed vegetables (like bell peppers and onions), cooked shrimp, etc.
- Olive oil or butter, for cooking

Instructions:

1. Prepare the fillings (if using):

- If you're adding any fillings such as cooked meats or vegetables, have them ready and set aside.

2. Assemble the quesadillas:

- Heat a large skillet or griddle over medium heat.
- Place one tortilla flat on the skillet. Sprinkle about 1/2 cup of shredded cheese evenly over the tortilla.
- If using additional fillings, add them on top of the cheese.
- Place another tortilla on top to cover the fillings, creating a sandwich.

3. Cook the quesadilla:

- Cook the quesadilla for about 2-3 minutes on each side, or until the tortilla is golden brown and crispy, and the cheese is melted. You can press down lightly with a spatula to help seal and cook evenly.

4. Repeat with remaining tortillas:

- Remove the cooked quesadilla from the skillet and place it on a cutting board. Allow it to cool for a minute before cutting into wedges.
- Repeat the process with the remaining tortillas and fillings.

5. Serve:

- Serve the quesadillas warm, garnished with toppings like salsa, guacamole, sour cream, or fresh cilantro if desired.

Tips:

- **Cheese:** Experiment with different types of cheese for varying flavors. A combination of cheeses works well too.
- **Variations:** Feel free to customize with your favorite fillings. You can also add spices like cumin, chili powder, or smoked paprika for extra flavor.
- **Cooking method:** Quesadillas can also be baked in the oven or cooked on a grill for a slightly different texture.

Quesadillas make for a quick and satisfying meal or snack, perfect for any time of day. They're versatile and can be adapted to suit your taste preferences or what you have on hand. Enjoy!

Arroz con Pollo (Chicken with Rice)

Ingredients:

- 2 lbs chicken pieces (bone-in, skin-on thighs and/or drumsticks)

- Salt and pepper, to taste
- 2 tablespoons vegetable oil or olive oil
- 1 onion, finely chopped
- 1 bell pepper (red or green), chopped
- 3 cloves garlic, minced
- 1 teaspoon ground cumin
- 1 teaspoon paprika
- 1/2 teaspoon dried oregano
- 1/2 teaspoon turmeric (optional, for color)
- 1 cup long-grain white rice
- 1 3/4 cups chicken broth
- 1/2 cup tomato sauce or crushed tomatoes
- 1 cup frozen peas (optional)
- Fresh cilantro or parsley, chopped (for garnish)
- Lime wedges (for serving)

Instructions:

1. Season and brown the chicken:

- Season the chicken pieces generously with salt and pepper.
- In a large skillet or Dutch oven, heat the vegetable oil over medium-high heat.
- Add the chicken pieces, skin side down, and cook until browned on both sides, about 5-7 minutes per side. Remove the chicken from the skillet and set aside.

2. Sauté the aromatics:

- In the same skillet, add the chopped onion and bell pepper. Cook until softened, about 5 minutes.
- Add the minced garlic, ground cumin, paprika, dried oregano, and turmeric (if using). Stir and cook for another 1-2 minutes until fragrant.

3. Cook the rice:

- Add the rice to the skillet and stir to coat with the onion and spice mixture.
- Pour in the chicken broth and tomato sauce (or crushed tomatoes). Stir well to combine.
- Nestle the browned chicken pieces back into the skillet, along with any juices that have accumulated.
- Bring to a simmer, then reduce the heat to low. Cover and cook for 20-25 minutes, or until the rice is tender and the chicken is cooked through. Stir occasionally to prevent sticking.

4. Add peas (optional) and finish:

- If using frozen peas, stir them into the skillet during the last 5 minutes of cooking.

- Taste and adjust seasoning with salt and pepper if needed.

5. Serve:

- Remove from heat and let the Arroz con Pollo sit, covered, for a few minutes before serving.
- Garnish with chopped fresh cilantro or parsley.
- Serve hot, accompanied by lime wedges for squeezing over the rice.

Tips:

- **Chicken:** You can use bone-in, skin-on chicken thighs, drumsticks, or a combination for more flavor. You can also use boneless, skinless chicken thighs if preferred.
- **Rice:** Long-grain white rice works best for this dish. Rinse the rice before using to remove excess starch if desired.
- **Variations:** Some recipes may include olives, capers, or raisins for added flavor and texture. Feel free to adjust according to your taste preferences.
- **Storage:** Arroz con Pollo stores well in the refrigerator for a few days and can be reheated on the stove or in the microwave.

Arroz con Pollo is a hearty one-pot meal that's perfect for family dinners or gatherings. It's comforting, aromatic, and full of delicious flavors that everyone will enjoy.

Fajitas

Ingredients:

- 1 pound boneless, skinless chicken breasts or thighs, thinly sliced
- 2 tablespoons olive oil

- 1 red bell pepper, thinly sliced
- 1 green bell pepper, thinly sliced
- 1 onion, thinly sliced
- 3 cloves garlic, minced
- 1 teaspoon chili powder
- 1 teaspoon ground cumin
- 1/2 teaspoon paprika
- 1/2 teaspoon garlic powder
- Salt and pepper, to taste
- Juice of 1 lime
- Fresh cilantro, chopped (optional, for garnish)
- Flour tortillas, for serving
- Optional toppings: sour cream, guacamole, salsa, shredded cheese

Instructions:

1. Marinate the chicken:

- In a bowl, combine the sliced chicken with olive oil, minced garlic, chili powder, ground cumin, paprika, garlic powder, salt, pepper, and lime juice. Mix well to coat the chicken evenly. Let it marinate for at least 15-20 minutes.

2. Prepare the vegetables:

- Heat a large skillet or grill pan over medium-high heat.
- Add a tablespoon of olive oil to the skillet.
- Add the sliced bell peppers and onion to the skillet. Sauté for 5-7 minutes, until they are tender and slightly caramelized. Remove the vegetables from the skillet and set aside.

3. Cook the chicken:

- In the same skillet, add the marinated chicken slices in a single layer.
- Cook for about 5-7 minutes, stirring occasionally, until the chicken is cooked through and nicely browned.

4. Combine and serve:

- Return the sautéed vegetables to the skillet with the cooked chicken. Stir everything together to combine and heat through.
- Taste and adjust seasoning with more salt, pepper, or lime juice if needed.

5. Serve the fajitas:

- Warm the flour tortillas either in the microwave wrapped in a damp paper towel or in a dry skillet for a few seconds on each side.
- Place a generous spoonful of the chicken and vegetable mixture onto each tortilla.

- Garnish with chopped fresh cilantro if desired.
- Serve immediately with optional toppings like sour cream, guacamole, salsa, and shredded cheese.

Tips:

- **Variations:** You can also make beef fajitas using thinly sliced skirt steak or flank steak. Adjust cooking times accordingly based on the type of meat you choose.
- **Vegetarian option:** Substitute the chicken with extra-firm tofu or portobello mushrooms for a vegetarian version.
- **Make-ahead:** You can marinate the chicken and prepare the vegetables ahead of time. Cook the fajitas just before serving for the best flavor and texture.
- **Leftovers:** Fajita leftovers can be stored in the refrigerator for a few days. Reheat in a skillet or microwave before serving.

Fajitas are versatile, flavorful, and perfect for a casual dinner or gathering. They're customizable with various toppings and fillings, making them a favorite for many Tex-Mex enthusiasts. Enjoy your homemade chicken fajitas!

Chile con Carne

Ingredients:

- 1 pound ground beef (or cubed beef chuck)
- 1 onion, chopped

- 3 cloves garlic, minced
- 1 bell pepper (any color), chopped
- 2-3 jalapeño peppers, seeded and finely chopped (adjust to taste)
- 2 tablespoons chili powder
- 1 teaspoon ground cumin
- 1 teaspoon paprika
- 1/2 teaspoon dried oregano
- 1/4 teaspoon cayenne pepper (optional, for extra heat)
- Salt and pepper, to taste
- 1 can (15 ounces) diced tomatoes
- 1 can (15 ounces) kidney beans, drained and rinsed (optional)
- 1 cup beef broth or water
- 1 tablespoon tomato paste (optional, for richer flavor)
- Chopped fresh cilantro or green onions, for garnish
- Sour cream, shredded cheese, sliced jalapeños, for serving (optional)
- Cornbread or warm tortillas, for serving (optional)

Instructions:

1. **Brown the beef:**
   - In a large pot or Dutch oven, brown the ground beef over medium-high heat until fully cooked and no longer pink. If using cubed beef chuck, brown the pieces in batches. Drain any excess fat if needed.
2. **Sauté aromatics:**
   - Add the chopped onion, minced garlic, bell pepper, and jalapeño peppers to the pot with the cooked beef. Sauté for about 5 minutes until the vegetables are softened.
3. **Add spices and tomatoes:**
   - Stir in the chili powder, ground cumin, paprika, dried oregano, cayenne pepper (if using), salt, and pepper. Cook for 1-2 minutes until the spices are fragrant.
   - Add the diced tomatoes (with their juices) to the pot. Stir well to combine.
4. **Simmer the chili:**
   - Pour in the beef broth (or water) and add the drained kidney beans (if using). Stir in the tomato paste for a richer flavor, if desired.
   - Bring the mixture to a boil, then reduce the heat to low. Cover and simmer for at least 30 minutes to allow the flavors to meld together, stirring occasionally. For deeper flavor, simmer for up to 1-2 hours, adding more broth or water if the chili becomes too thick.
5. **Serve:**
   - Taste and adjust seasoning with more salt and pepper if needed.
   - Ladle the chili into bowls and garnish with chopped fresh cilantro or green onions.
   - Serve hot with optional toppings like sour cream, shredded cheese, and sliced jalapeños. Enjoy with cornbread or warm tortillas on the side.

Tips:

- **Variations:** Customize your chili by adding different types of beans (black beans, pinto beans) or adjusting the level of heat with more or fewer jalapeños and cayenne pepper.
- **Storage:** Chili con carne develops even richer flavors the next day. Store leftovers in an airtight container in the refrigerator for up to 3-4 days, or freeze for longer storage.
- **Serving ideas:** Besides serving in bowls, chili con carne is versatile and can be served over baked potatoes, hot dogs, or used as a filling for tacos and burritos.

This hearty chili con carne recipe is perfect for warming up on chilly days or for casual gatherings. Enjoy making and sharing this delicious dish!

Tostadas

Ingredients:

- 6 corn tortillas
- Vegetable oil, for frying
- 1 pound ground beef

- 1 small onion, finely chopped
- 2 cloves garlic, minced
- 1 tablespoon chili powder
- 1 teaspoon ground cumin
- 1/2 teaspoon paprika
- Salt and pepper, to taste
- 1 can (15 ounces) refried beans
- Shredded lettuce
- Diced tomatoes
- Sliced jalapeños (optional)
- Shredded cheese (such as cheddar or Monterey Jack)
- Sour cream, guacamole, or salsa, for topping
- Fresh cilantro, chopped, for garnish

Instructions:

1. Prepare the tortillas:

- In a large skillet, heat about 1/2 inch of vegetable oil over medium-high heat until hot but not smoking.
- Fry each tortilla one at a time, turning once, until crisp and golden brown, about 1-2 minutes per side. Drain on paper towels.

2. Cook the beef mixture:

- In a separate skillet, cook the ground beef over medium-high heat until browned and cooked through, breaking it up with a spoon as it cooks.
- Add the chopped onion and minced garlic to the skillet with the beef. Cook for 2-3 minutes until the onion is softened.
- Stir in the chili powder, ground cumin, paprika, salt, and pepper. Cook for another minute until fragrant. Remove from heat.

3. Heat the refried beans:

- In a small saucepan, heat the refried beans over medium heat until warmed through, stirring occasionally.

4. Assemble the tostadas:

- Spread a layer of warm refried beans onto each crispy tortilla.
- Top with a generous spoonful of the beef mixture.
- Add shredded lettuce, diced tomatoes, sliced jalapeños (if using), and shredded cheese on top.

5. Serve:

- Garnish with a dollop of sour cream, guacamole, or salsa.
- Sprinkle with chopped fresh cilantro for added freshness.
- Serve immediately while warm and crispy.

Tips:

- **Variations:** You can customize your tostadas with different toppings such as shredded chicken, pork, or even seafood like shrimp or fish.
- **Baking option:** If you prefer not to fry the tortillas, you can bake them in the oven until crispy. Brush each tortilla lightly with oil on both sides and bake at 400°F (200°C) for about 5-7 minutes per side until crisp.
- **Make it vegetarian:** Skip the ground beef and use seasoned black beans or grilled vegetables as a filling.
- **Storage:** Tostadas are best enjoyed fresh to maintain their crispiness. You can prepare all the components ahead of time and assemble just before serving.

Tostadas are versatile and make for a delicious appetizer or main dish. They're perfect for a casual meal or for entertaining guests with a build-your-own tostada bar. Enjoy creating and savoring these crispy and flavorful treats!

Pico de Gallo

Ingredients:

- 4 ripe tomatoes, diced
- 1/2 onion, finely chopped

- 1-2 jalapeño or serrano peppers, seeded and finely chopped (adjust to taste)
- 1/2 cup chopped fresh cilantro leaves
- Juice of 1-2 limes (about 2-3 tablespoons)
- Salt, to taste

Instructions:

1. **Prepare the ingredients:**
   - Dice the tomatoes into small pieces. If desired, you can deseed them to reduce the moisture content.
   - Finely chop the onion and jalapeño or serrano peppers. For a spicier salsa, leave the seeds and membranes intact; for milder salsa, remove them.
   - Chop the fresh cilantro leaves.
2. **Combine the ingredients:**
   - In a mixing bowl, combine the diced tomatoes, chopped onion, chopped peppers, and chopped cilantro.
3. **Season with lime juice and salt:**
   - Squeeze fresh lime juice over the mixture. Start with the juice of one lime and adjust to taste. The lime juice adds acidity and enhances the flavors of the salsa.
   - Season with salt, starting with a pinch, and adjust to taste. The salt helps to bring out the flavors of the other ingredients.
4. **Mix well and let it marinate:**
   - Gently toss all the ingredients together until well combined.
   - Let the Pico de Gallo sit at room temperature for about 15-30 minutes before serving to allow the flavors to meld together.
5. **Serve:**
   - Serve Pico de Gallo fresh as a topping or dip alongside your favorite Mexican dishes such as tacos, quesadillas, fajitas, or grilled meats.
   - It can also be enjoyed with tortilla chips as a refreshing snack.

Tips:

- **Customize:** Feel free to adjust the quantities of ingredients to suit your taste preferences. You can add more or less onion, peppers, or cilantro based on your liking.
- **Storage:** Pico de Gallo is best enjoyed fresh. Store any leftovers in an airtight container in the refrigerator for up to 2-3 days. Stir well before serving again.
- **Variations:** Add diced avocado or mango for a twist on traditional Pico de Gallo. You can also experiment with different types of peppers or herbs for unique flavors.

Pico de Gallo is simple to make and adds a burst of freshness and color to your meals. It's a must-have condiment for any Mexican-inspired cuisine and is sure to brighten up your table with its vibrant flavors.

Birria

Ingredients:

For the Birria:

- 3 lbs beef chuck roast or brisket, cut into large chunks
- 1 onion, chopped
- 4 cloves garlic, minced
- 2 bay leaves
- 1 tablespoon dried oregano
- 1 tablespoon ground cumin
- 1 teaspoon ground coriander
- 1 teaspoon smoked paprika (optional)
- 1/2 teaspoon ground cloves
- 1/2 teaspoon ground cinnamon
- Salt and pepper, to taste
- 2 cups beef broth
- 2 cups water
- 1 cup tomato sauce or crushed tomatoes
- 1/4 cup apple cider vinegar or white vinegar
- Corn tortillas, for serving

For Serving (Optional):

- Chopped fresh cilantro
- Diced onions
- Lime wedges
- Sliced radishes
- Salsa or hot sauce

Instructions:

1. **Prepare the Beef:**
   - Season the beef chunks generously with salt and pepper.
2. **Sear the Beef:**
   - Heat a large Dutch oven or heavy-bottomed pot over medium-high heat.
   - Add the beef chunks in batches and sear until browned on all sides. This step helps develop flavor. Remove and set aside.
3. **Make the Birria Sauce:**
   - In the same pot, add chopped onion and cook until softened, about 5 minutes.
   - Add minced garlic, bay leaves, dried oregano, ground cumin, ground coriander, smoked paprika (if using), ground cloves, and ground cinnamon. Cook for 1-2 minutes until fragrant.
4. **Combine and Simmer:**
   - Return the seared beef chunks back to the pot.
   - Pour in beef broth, water, tomato sauce or crushed tomatoes, and apple cider vinegar (or white vinegar). Stir to combine.
   - Bring to a boil, then reduce heat to low. Cover and simmer gently for 2.5 to 3 hours, or until the beef is very tender and falls apart easily.
5. **Shred the Beef:**

- Once the beef is tender, remove it from the pot and shred it using two forks. Return the shredded beef back to the pot and stir to combine with the sauce.
6. **Serve the Birria:**
    - Serve the birria in bowls, with warm corn tortillas on the side for dipping or wrapping.
    - Optionally, garnish with chopped fresh cilantro, diced onions, lime wedges, sliced radishes, and salsa or hot sauce.

Tips:

- **Meat Selection:** You can use beef chuck roast or brisket for this recipe. These cuts are ideal because they become tender and flavorful when slow-cooked.
- **Make-Ahead:** Birria tastes even better the next day as the flavors meld. It can be stored in the refrigerator for up to 3-4 days.
- **Variations:** Some recipes include adding dried chilies for a richer, spicier broth. You can adjust the level of heat and spices to suit your taste.

Birria de Res is a comforting and delicious dish, perfect for gatherings or special occasions. Its rich, flavorful broth and tender beef make it a favorite among Mexican cuisine enthusiasts. Enjoy this traditional recipe with your favorite toppings and sides!

Flan

Ingredients:

- **For the caramel:**

- 1 cup granulated sugar
- 1/4 cup water
- **For the custard:**
    - 1 can (14 oz) sweetened condensed milk
    - 1 can (12 oz) evaporated milk
    - 4 large eggs
    - 1 teaspoon vanilla extract

Instructions:

1. **Prepare the caramel:**
    - In a heavy-bottomed saucepan, combine the sugar and water over medium-high heat.
    - Stir until the sugar dissolves.
    - Stop stirring and let the mixture boil until it turns a golden amber color, swirling the pan occasionally to ensure even caramelization.
    - Once caramelized, immediately pour it into a 9-inch round baking dish or individual ramekins, swirling to coat the bottom evenly. Be careful as the caramel will be extremely hot.
2. **Preheat the oven:**
    - Preheat your oven to 350°F (175°C) and place a larger baking dish filled with about 1 inch of hot water into the oven. This will be used as a water bath (bain-marie) for baking the flan.
3. **Make the custard:**
    - In a large bowl, whisk together the sweetened condensed milk, evaporated milk, eggs, and vanilla extract until smooth and well combined.
4. **Assemble and bake:**
    - Carefully pour the custard mixture over the caramel in the baking dish or ramekins.
    - Place the filled baking dish or ramekins into the larger baking dish with hot water (water bath).
5. **Bake the flan:**
    - Bake in the preheated oven for about 45-55 minutes for a large dish or 30-40 minutes for individual ramekins, or until the custard is set around the edges but still slightly jiggly in the center.
6. **Chill and serve:**
    - Remove the flan from the water bath and let it cool to room temperature.
    - Once cooled, cover and refrigerate for at least 4 hours or overnight to allow the flan to set completely.
7. **Serve:**
    - To serve, run a knife around the edges of the flan to loosen it from the dish.
    - Place a serving plate upside down over the baking dish or ramekin and quickly invert to release the flan onto the plate, allowing the caramel to drizzle over the top.

8. **Enjoy:**
    - Slice and serve the flan chilled, garnished with fresh berries or whipped cream if desired.

Flan is best enjoyed chilled and can be kept refrigerated for a few days. It's a deliciously smooth and creamy dessert with a beautiful caramel flavor that's sure to impress!

Churros

Ingredients:

- 1 cup water

- 2 tablespoons white sugar
- 1/2 teaspoon salt
- 2 tablespoons vegetable oil
- 1 cup all-purpose flour
- Vegetable oil, for frying
- 1/2 cup white sugar (for coating)
- 1 teaspoon ground cinnamon (for coating)

Instructions:

1. **Prepare the dough:**
   - In a small saucepan over medium heat, combine water, sugar, salt, and vegetable oil. Bring to a boil and remove from heat.
   - Stir in the flour until the mixture forms a ball. It should pull away from the sides of the pan.
2. **Fry the churros:**
   - Heat vegetable oil in a large, deep skillet or pot until it reaches 375°F (190°C).
   - Spoon the dough into a piping bag fitted with a large star tip. Pipe 4-6 inch strips of dough into the hot oil, cutting them with scissors. Be careful not to overcrowd the pan.
   - Fry until golden brown, about 2-4 minutes per side. Remove from oil and drain on paper towels briefly.
3. **Coat the churros:**
   - In a shallow dish, combine 1/2 cup sugar and cinnamon.
   - Roll the warm churros in the cinnamon-sugar mixture until evenly coated.
4. **Serve:**
   - Serve churros warm with a dipping sauce of your choice, such as chocolate sauce, dulce de leche, or caramel.

Enjoy these homemade churros as a delightful dessert or sweet snack! They are best enjoyed fresh and warm, straight from the frying pan.

Empanadas

Dough Ingredients:

- 3 cups all-purpose flour

- 1 teaspoon salt
- 1/2 cup (1 stick) cold unsalted butter, cut into small pieces
- 1 large egg
- 1/2 - 3/4 cup cold water

Filling Ingredients (Beef Empanadas):

- 1 tablespoon olive oil
- 1 small onion, finely chopped
- 2 cloves garlic, minced
- 1/2 red bell pepper, finely chopped
- 1/2 green bell pepper, finely chopped
- 1/2 teaspoon ground cumin
- 1/2 teaspoon paprika
- 1/4 teaspoon chili powder (optional)
- Salt and pepper to taste
- 1/2 lb ground beef
- 1/4 cup tomato sauce or diced tomatoes
- 2 tablespoons chopped fresh cilantro or parsley (optional)
- 12 pitted green olives, chopped (optional)
- 2 hard-boiled eggs, chopped (optional)

Instructions:

1. **Prepare the dough:**
   - In a large bowl, combine the flour and salt.
   - Cut in the cold butter using a pastry cutter or your fingers until the mixture resembles coarse crumbs.
   - In a small bowl, whisk together the egg and 1/2 cup cold water.
   - Gradually add the egg mixture to the flour mixture, stirring with a fork until the dough begins to come together. Add more water, 1 tablespoon at a time, if needed.
   - Turn the dough out onto a lightly floured surface and knead gently until smooth. Wrap in plastic wrap and refrigerate for at least 30 minutes.
2. **Prepare the filling:**
   - Heat olive oil in a large skillet over medium heat. Add onion and cook until translucent, about 3-4 minutes.
   - Add garlic, red bell pepper, and green bell pepper. Cook for another 2-3 minutes until peppers are softened.
   - Stir in ground cumin, paprika, chili powder (if using), salt, and pepper.
   - Add ground beef and cook until browned and cooked through, breaking it up with a spoon.
   - Stir in tomato sauce or diced tomatoes and cook for another 2-3 minutes.

- Remove from heat and stir in chopped cilantro or parsley, chopped olives (if using), and chopped hard-boiled eggs (if using). Let the filling cool completely.

3. **Assemble the empanadas:**
    - Preheat oven to 375°F (190°C). Line a baking sheet with parchment paper.
    - Divide the dough into 12 equal portions. Roll each portion into a ball and flatten into a disk on a lightly floured surface.
    - Roll out each disk into a circle about 6-7 inches in diameter, using a rolling pin.

4. **Fill and fold the empanadas:**
    - Spoon about 2 tablespoons of filling onto the center of each dough circle.
    - Fold the dough over the filling to create a half-moon shape. Press the edges together with your fingers to seal. You can crimp the edges with a fork for a decorative touch.

5. **Bake the empanadas:**
    - Place the assembled empanadas on the prepared baking sheet.
    - Brush the tops with beaten egg or milk for a golden finish (optional).
    - Bake for 20-25 minutes, or until golden brown and crispy.

6. **Serve:**
    - Let the empanadas cool slightly before serving. They can be enjoyed warm or at room temperature.

These beef empanadas are delicious as a snack, appetizer, or even a main course. You can customize the filling based on your preferences or dietary needs. Enjoy making and eating these flavorful treats!

Aguachile

Ingredients:

- 1 lb fresh shrimp, peeled and deveined
- 1 cup fresh lime juice (about 8-10 limes)
- 1 cucumber, thinly sliced
- 1/2 red onion, thinly sliced
- 1-2 serrano chilies (or to taste), thinly sliced
- 1/2 cup chopped fresh cilantro
- Salt to taste
- Tortilla chips or tostadas, for serving

Instructions:

1. **Prepare the shrimp:**
    - Rinse the shrimp under cold water and pat dry with paper towels.
    - If desired, slice the shrimp in half lengthwise to make them thinner (this is optional).
2. **Marinate the shrimp:**
    - In a glass or ceramic bowl, combine the shrimp and lime juice. Make sure the shrimp are completely covered in the lime juice.
    - Cover the bowl and refrigerate for about 15-20 minutes. The lime juice will "cook" the shrimp slightly, turning them opaque and firm.
3. **Prepare the sauce:**
    - In a blender or food processor, combine the sliced serrano chilies, cilantro, and a pinch of salt.
    - Blend until smooth. Taste and adjust salt if needed.
4. **Assemble the aguachile:**
    - Drain most of the lime juice from the shrimp, leaving just a little to keep them moist.
    - Add the sliced cucumber, red onion, and the blended chili-cilantro sauce to the shrimp.
    - Gently toss everything together until well combined and evenly coated.
5. **Chill and serve:**
    - Cover the bowl again and refrigerate for at least 15-30 minutes to allow the flavors to meld together and the shrimp to absorb the sauce.
6. **Serve:**
    - Serve aguachile cold, garnished with additional cilantro if desired.
    - Accompany with tortilla chips or tostadas for scooping up the shrimp and sauce.

Aguachile is typically enjoyed as a starter or appetizer due to its refreshing and spicy flavors. It's perfect for hot days when you're craving something zesty and light. Adjust the spiciness by adding more or less serrano chilies according to your preference. Enjoy this vibrant dish straight from the coastal regions of Mexico!

Camarones a la Diabla (Spicy Shrimp)

Ingredients:

- 1 lb large shrimp, peeled and deveined
- 3 dried guajillo chilies

- 3 dried arbol chilies (adjust based on your spice preference)
- 2 tomatoes, diced
- 1/2 onion, diced
- 3 garlic cloves, minced
- 1/4 cup chicken or vegetable broth
- 2 tablespoons vegetable oil
- 1 tablespoon tomato paste
- 1 teaspoon dried oregano
- 1/2 teaspoon ground cumin
- Salt and pepper to taste
- Lime wedges and chopped cilantro for garnish
- Cooked rice or warm tortillas, for serving

Instructions:

1. **Prepare the dried chilies:**
   - Remove the stems and seeds from the dried guajillo and arbol chilies.
   - Heat a dry skillet over medium heat and toast the chilies for about 1-2 minutes per side until they become fragrant and slightly blistered. Be careful not to burn them.
   - Place the toasted chilies in a bowl and cover with hot water. Let them soak for about 15-20 minutes until softened.
2. **Make the chili sauce:**
   - Drain the soaked chilies and transfer them to a blender.
   - Add the diced tomatoes, onion, garlic, tomato paste, dried oregano, ground cumin, salt, pepper, and chicken or vegetable broth.
   - Blend until smooth. If needed, add a bit more broth or water to achieve a sauce-like consistency.
3. **Cook the shrimp:**
   - In a large skillet or frying pan, heat the vegetable oil over medium-high heat.
   - Add the shrimp and cook for about 2-3 minutes per side until they turn pink and opaque. Remove the shrimp from the pan and set aside.
4. **Simmer the sauce:**
   - In the same skillet, add the blended chili sauce. Bring it to a simmer over medium heat.
   - Cook the sauce for about 5-7 minutes, stirring occasionally, until it thickens slightly and deepens in color.
5. **Combine shrimp and sauce:**
   - Add the cooked shrimp back into the skillet with the sauce. Stir gently to coat the shrimp evenly with the sauce.
   - Let it simmer together for another 2-3 minutes to allow the flavors to meld.
6. **Serve:**
   - Serve Camarones a la Diabla hot, garnished with chopped cilantro and lime wedges.

- Serve with cooked rice or warm tortillas on the side to soak up the delicious sauce.

Camarones a la Diabla is a spicy and satisfying dish that pairs well with rice, beans, or a fresh salad. Adjust the amount of arbol chilies to control the spiciness level according to your preference. Enjoy this flavorful Mexican shrimp dish with family and friends!

Cochinita Pibil

Ingredients:

- 2 lbs pork shoulder, cut into 2-inch cubes

- 4 oz achiote paste (annatto paste)
- 1/2 cup orange juice (freshly squeezed if possible)
- 1/4 cup lime juice (freshly squeezed if possible)
- 3 cloves garlic, minced
- 1 teaspoon ground cumin
- 1 teaspoon dried oregano
- 1/2 teaspoon ground cinnamon
- 1/2 teaspoon ground allspice
- 1/2 teaspoon ground cloves
- Salt and pepper to taste
- Banana leaves (optional, for wrapping)
- Sliced red onion and cilantro, for garnish
- Warm tortillas, for serving

Instructions:

1. **Prepare the marinade:**
   - In a blender or food processor, combine the achiote paste, orange juice, lime juice, minced garlic, ground cumin, dried oregano, ground cinnamon, ground allspice, ground cloves, salt, and pepper.
   - Blend until smooth to form the marinade.
2. **Marinate the pork:**
   - Place the pork cubes in a large bowl or resealable plastic bag.
   - Pour the marinade over the pork, making sure each piece is well coated.
   - Cover or seal and refrigerate for at least 4 hours, preferably overnight, to allow the flavors to penetrate the meat.
3. **Cooking options:**
   - **Traditional method (using banana leaves):**
     - Preheat your oven to 325°F (160°C).
     - If using banana leaves, briefly pass them over an open flame to soften them and enhance their flavor. Line a baking dish with banana leaves, allowing them to hang over the sides.
     - Place the marinated pork and marinade in the lined baking dish. Fold the banana leaves over the top to enclose the pork completely.
     - Cover tightly with foil and bake in the preheated oven for about 3-4 hours, or until the pork is very tender and easily shreds with a fork.
   - **Alternative method (using a slow cooker or instant pot):**
     - Transfer the marinated pork and marinade to a slow cooker or instant pot.
     - Cook on low for 6-8 hours in a slow cooker or on the "slow cook" setting in an instant pot until the pork is tender and easily shreds.
4. **Serve:**
   - Once the pork is cooked, remove it from the oven or slow cooker.
   - Shred the pork using two forks.
   - Serve Cochinita Pibil warm, garnished with sliced red onion and cilantro.

- Serve with warm tortillas for making tacos or as a filling for sandwiches.

Cochinita Pibil is typically served with pickled red onions, which add a tangy contrast to the rich and flavorful pork. It's a delicious and aromatic dish that's sure to impress with its depth of flavors and tender texture. Enjoy this taste of Yucatán cuisine!

Elote (Mexican Street Corn)

Ingredients:

- Fresh corn on the cob
- Mayonnaise or Mexican crema (sour cream can be used as a substitute)

- Cotija cheese (or queso fresco as an alternative)
- Chili powder or Tajín seasoning
- Fresh lime wedges
- Optional: chopped cilantro, chopped green onions, hot sauce

Instructions:

1. **Grill or Boil the Corn:**
   - Start by grilling or boiling the corn until it's cooked through and slightly charred. Grilling gives it a smoky flavor, which adds to the dish's appeal.
2. **Coat with Mayonnaise or Crema:**
   - Once the corn is cooked, spread a layer of mayonnaise or Mexican crema all over each cob. This helps the other ingredients stick and adds a creamy texture.
3. **Sprinkle with Cheese:**
   - Roll the mayonnaise-coated corn in crumbled Cotija cheese (or queso fresco), ensuring it's evenly coated. The cheese adds a salty and tangy element.
4. **Season with Chili Powder or Tajín:**
   - Sprinkle chili powder or Tajín seasoning generously over the corn. This seasoning provides a spicy, tangy kick that complements the sweetness of the corn and richness of the cheese.
5. **Serve with Lime Wedges:**
   - Serve the elote hot, accompanied by fresh lime wedges. Squeezing lime juice over the corn just before eating adds a refreshing citrusy flavor.
6. **Optional Garnishes:**
   - For extra flavor and color, you can garnish with chopped cilantro, green onions, or a drizzle of hot sauce according to your taste preferences.

Enjoying Elote:

Elote is typically enjoyed as a street food snack in Mexico, served on a stick or with the husk as a handle. It's a perfect combination of creamy, tangy, spicy, and sweet flavors, making it a favorite at festivals, markets, and gatherings.

Huevos Rancheros

Ingredients:

- Corn tortillas (2 per serving)
- Eggs (2 per serving)

- Refried beans
- Salsa (homemade or store-bought)
- Chopped fresh cilantro (for garnish)
- Chopped onions (optional, for garnish)
- Sliced avocado (optional, for garnish)
- Queso fresco or shredded cheese (optional, for topping)
- Salt and pepper to taste

Instructions:

1. **Prepare the Tortillas:**
   - Warm the corn tortillas either by heating them in a dry skillet for a minute on each side or wrapping them in a damp paper towel and microwaving for 20-30 seconds. Keep them warm in a clean kitchen towel.
2. **Cook the Eggs:**
   - You have a few options for how to cook the eggs:
     - Fried Eggs: Heat a small amount of oil in a skillet over medium heat. Crack the eggs into the skillet and cook until the whites are set but the yolks are still runny, about 3-4 minutes.
     - Scrambled Eggs: Whisk the eggs in a bowl with a pinch of salt and pepper. Cook in a skillet over medium heat, stirring gently until just set.
3. **Warm the Refried Beans:**
   - Heat the refried beans in a small saucepan over medium-low heat until warmed through. You can add a little water or broth if they seem too thick.
4. **Assemble the Dish:**
   - Place a warm tortilla on a plate. Spread a generous spoonful of refried beans over the tortilla.
   - Place the cooked eggs on top of the beans.
5. **Add Salsa and Garnishes:**
   - Spoon salsa over the eggs. You can use mild or spicy salsa, depending on your preference.
   - Garnish with chopped cilantro, onions, avocado slices, and queso fresco or shredded cheese if desired.
6. **Serve Immediately:**
   - Serve the huevos rancheros immediately while everything is warm and fresh. The combination of flavors and textures is best enjoyed right away.

Notes:

- **Variations:** Some variations include adding a layer of sautéed vegetables (like bell peppers or onions) between the tortilla and beans, or topping with sour cream or guacamole.
- **Side Dish:** Huevos rancheros is often served with a side of Mexican rice or fried potatoes to make it a more substantial meal.

- **Customization:** Feel free to adjust the toppings and seasonings to suit your taste preferences. Some like it spicy with extra hot sauce, while others prefer a milder version.

Huevos rancheros is a versatile dish that can be enjoyed for breakfast, brunch, or even a hearty dinner. It captures the essence of Mexican flavors and is sure to satisfy your appetite!

Tlayudas

Ingredients:

- Large corn tortillas (about 10-12 inches in diameter)
- Refried black beans (you can make your own or use canned)
- Oaxaca cheese or shredded mozzarella cheese
- Shredded cooked chicken, beef, or pork (optional)
- Sliced avocado or guacamole
- Sliced tomatoes
- Thinly sliced red onion
- Chopped cilantro
- Salsa (preferably a spicy salsa such as salsa verde or salsa roja)
- Mexican crema or sour cream
- Salt and pepper to taste

Instructions:

1. **Prepare the Tortillas:**
   - Heat a large skillet or griddle over medium-high heat. Place one tortilla at a time on the skillet and heat for about 1-2 minutes on each side until it becomes slightly crispy and lightly browned. Repeat for each tortilla. Alternatively, you can grill the tortillas if you prefer.
2. **Spread the Beans:**
   - Spread a generous layer of refried black beans over each tortilla. Ensure the beans go all the way to the edges.
3. **Add Cheese and Toppings:**
   - Sprinkle shredded Oaxaca cheese or mozzarella cheese evenly over the beans while the tortilla is still hot so that it melts slightly. Add any optional toppings such as shredded chicken, beef, or pork if desired.
4. **Layer with Fresh Ingredients:**
   - Arrange sliced avocado or guacamole, sliced tomatoes, and thinly sliced red onion on top of the cheese and beans.
5. **Season and Garnish:**
   - Season with salt and pepper to taste. Sprinkle chopped cilantro over the tlayudas for freshness and added flavor.
6. **Serve with Salsa and Crema:**
   - Drizzle salsa generously over the tlayudas. You can choose a spicy salsa for extra kick or a milder one if preferred. Finish by drizzling Mexican crema or sour cream over the top.
7. **Slice and Serve:**
   - Cut the tlayudas into wedges, similar to pizza slices. Serve immediately while warm.

Tips:

- **Variations:** Tlayudas can be customized with various toppings such as chorizo, grilled vegetables, or even chapulines (crispy grasshoppers) for a traditional Oaxacan touch.

- **Cooking Method:** If you have access to a comal (a traditional Mexican griddle), it can impart a more authentic flavor to the tortillas.
- **Storage:** Tlayudas are best enjoyed fresh and hot. If you have leftovers, store the components separately and assemble just before serving to maintain the crispy texture of the tortilla.

Tlayudas are not only delicious but also a great way to explore the rich culinary heritage of Oaxaca. Enjoy these flavorful and hearty Mexican treats with family and friends!

Molletes

Ingredients:

- Bolillos or French bread rolls (you can also use baguettes or similar bread)

- Refried beans (traditionally made with pinto beans)
- Cheese (commonly used is Oaxaca cheese, but you can also use Monterey Jack, mozzarella, or any melting cheese)
- Salsa (salsa verde or salsa roja)
- Butter or olive oil
- Optional toppings: sliced jalapeños, chopped cilantro, avocado slices, Mexican crema or sour cream

Instructions:

1. **Prepare the Bread:**
   - Preheat your oven to 350°F (175°C).
   - Slice the bolillos or French bread rolls in half horizontally to create two halves per roll.
2. **Toast the Bread:**
   - Lightly butter or brush olive oil on the cut sides of the bread halves.
   - Place them cut-side up on a baking sheet and toast in the preheated oven for about 5-7 minutes, or until they are lightly crispy and golden brown.
3. **Spread the Beans:**
   - While the bread is toasting, heat the refried beans in a small saucepan until warmed through. You can add a little water or broth to loosen them up if needed.
   - Spread a generous layer of refried beans on each toasted bread half.
4. **Add Cheese:**
   - Sprinkle shredded cheese (Oaxaca, Monterey Jack, mozzarella, or your choice of melting cheese) evenly over the refried beans on each bread half.
5. **Broil or Bake:**
   - Place the assembled molletes back in the oven under the broiler for 2-3 minutes, or until the cheese is melted and bubbly. Alternatively, you can bake them at 350°F (175°C) for about 5-7 minutes until the cheese is melted.
6. **Serve with Salsa:**
   - Remove the molletes from the oven and transfer them to a serving plate.
   - Serve them hot, topped with salsa verde or salsa roja. You can spoon the salsa over the molletes or serve it on the side for dipping.
7. **Garnish and Enjoy:**
   - Optionally, garnish with sliced jalapeños, chopped cilantro, avocado slices, and a drizzle of Mexican crema or sour cream according to your preference.

Tips:

- **Variations:** You can customize molletes by adding cooked chorizo, sliced ham, or grilled vegetables on top of the beans and cheese before baking.
- **Storage:** Molletes are best enjoyed fresh and hot. If you have leftovers, store the components separately and assemble just before serving to maintain the texture of the bread.

Molletes are a comforting and versatile dish that combines the flavors of beans, melted cheese, and salsa on toasted bread—a perfect way to start your day or as a snack any time!

Papas con Chorizo (Potatoes with Chorizo)

Ingredients:

- 2-3 medium potatoes, peeled and diced into small cubes

- 1/2 lb (about 225g) Mexican chorizo sausage, removed from casings if necessary
- 1/2 onion, finely chopped
- 1-2 cloves garlic, minced
- 1-2 tomatoes, diced (optional)
- Fresh cilantro, chopped (for garnish)
- Salt and pepper to taste
- Optional toppings: crumbled queso fresco, avocado slices, salsa

Instructions:

1. **Prepare the Potatoes:**
   - Peel the potatoes and dice them into small cubes. Rinse them under cold water to remove excess starch.
2. **Cook the Potatoes:**
   - Heat a large skillet or frying pan over medium heat. Add a tablespoon of oil (vegetable or olive oil) and sauté the diced potatoes until they are golden brown and cooked through, about 10-15 minutes. Stir occasionally to ensure even cooking. Remove the potatoes from the skillet and set aside.
3. **Cook the Chorizo:**
   - In the same skillet, add the chorizo sausage. Break it up with a spoon and cook it over medium heat until it's fully cooked and browned, about 5-7 minutes. If there's excess fat, you can drain some of it, but leave a bit for flavor.
4. **Add Aromatics:**
   - Add the chopped onion to the skillet with the chorizo and cook until the onion is softened and translucent, about 3-4 minutes. Stir in the minced garlic and cook for another minute until fragrant.
5. **Combine Potatoes and Chorizo:**
   - Return the cooked potatoes to the skillet with the chorizo mixture. Stir everything together gently to combine. If you like, you can add diced tomatoes at this stage for extra flavor and moisture. Cook for another 2-3 minutes until everything is heated through.
6. **Season and Garnish:**
   - Season the papas con chorizo with salt and pepper to taste. Sprinkle fresh chopped cilantro over the top for garnish.
7. **Serve Hot:**
   - Serve papas con chorizo hot, either on its own or with warm tortillas on the side. You can also top it with crumbled queso fresco, avocado slices, or salsa for extra flavor.

Tips:

- **Variations:** Some recipes include adding diced bell peppers or jalapeños for extra heat and flavor. You can also adjust the spiciness by choosing mild or spicy chorizo.

- **Storage:** Papas con chorizo can be stored in the refrigerator for up to 3 days. Reheat gently on the stove or in the microwave before serving.

Papas con Chorizo is a comforting and satisfying dish that brings together the rich flavors of chorizo and potatoes. It's perfect for a leisurely breakfast or brunch, served with warm tortillas or crusty bread. Enjoy the deliciousness of Mexican cuisine with this flavorful dish!

Sopes

Ingredients:

- 2 cups masa harina (corn flour)
- 1 1/4 cups warm water
- Pinch of salt
- Vegetable oil, for frying

For Toppings (choose any combination):

- Refried beans
- Cooked and shredded chicken, beef, or pork
- Lettuce, shredded
- Mexican crema or sour cream
- Queso fresco or shredded cheese
- Salsa (salsa verde or salsa roja)
- Diced tomatoes
- Sliced avocado or guacamole
- Chopped cilantro
- Sliced jalapeños

Instructions:

1. **Prepare the Dough:**
   - In a large bowl, combine the masa harina and salt. Gradually add the warm water, mixing with your hands until a soft dough forms. The dough should be smooth and pliable, similar to Play-Doh consistency.
2. **Form the Sopes:**
   - Pinch off a golf ball-sized piece of dough and roll it into a ball. Flatten the ball between your palms to form a disc about 1/4 inch thick. Use your thumbs to create a rim or edge around the disc, pressing slightly to form a shallow well in the center. Repeat with the remaining dough.
3. **Cook the Sopes:**
   - Heat a skillet or griddle over medium-high heat. Lightly grease the skillet with vegetable oil. Place the sopes on the skillet and cook for about 2-3 minutes on each side, or until they are lightly browned and cooked through. Press down gently with a spatula while cooking to ensure even browning.
4. **Fry the Sopes (optional):**
   - For extra crispiness, you can fry the sopes after cooking them on the skillet. Heat about 1/2 inch of vegetable oil in a frying pan over medium heat. Carefully place the sopes in the hot oil and fry for about 1-2 minutes on each side until golden and crispy. Drain on paper towels.
5. **Top the Sopes:**
   - Once the sopes are cooked and crispy, spread a layer of refried beans on each one, covering the bottom and up to the edges.

- Add your choice of toppings such as cooked and shredded meat, shredded lettuce, salsa, cheese, diced tomatoes, sliced avocado or guacamole, Mexican crema or sour cream, chopped cilantro, and sliced jalapeños.
6. **Serve Immediately:**
    - Arrange the prepared sopes on a serving platter and serve immediately while they are warm and crispy. Enjoy as a delicious appetizer or snack.

Tips:

- **Customization:** Sopes are highly customizable. You can vary the toppings based on your preferences or what you have on hand.
- **Make-Ahead:** You can prepare the sopes ahead of time and store them in an airtight container at room temperature. Reheat in a toaster oven or oven before adding the toppings.
- **Variations:** Some recipes call for adding a layer of lettuce or cabbage between the beans and other toppings for added crunch and freshness.

Sopes are a delightful way to experience the flavors and textures of Mexican cuisine. Whether you enjoy them as a snack, appetizer, or part of a meal, they are sure to be a hit with their crispy base and delicious toppings!

Champurrado (Mexican Hot Chocolate)

Ingredients:

- 4 cups water
- 1 cinnamon stick
- 2 cups milk (whole milk or evaporated milk for richer flavor)
- 1/2 cup masa harina (corn flour)
- 1/2 cup piloncillo (Mexican brown sugar) or granulated sugar (adjust to taste)
- 2-3 tbsp cocoa powder
- 1/2 tsp ground cinnamon (optional)
- Pinch of salt
- Mexican chocolate tablet (optional, for extra richness and flavor)
- Vanilla extract (optional)
- Whipped cream (optional, for serving)
- Ground cinnamon or cocoa powder, for garnish

Instructions:

1. **Prepare the Cinnamon Water:**
   - In a medium saucepan, bring 4 cups of water and the cinnamon stick to a boil. Reduce the heat and simmer for about 10 minutes to infuse the water with cinnamon flavor. Remove the cinnamon stick and discard.
2. **Mix the Masa Slurry:**
   - In a small bowl, whisk together the masa harina with 1 cup of the milk until smooth. This helps to prevent lumps when you add it to the hot liquid.
3. **Prepare the Champurrado Base:**
   - Gradually pour the masa harina mixture into the cinnamon-infused water, stirring constantly to prevent lumps. Add the remaining 1 cup of milk and continue stirring until well combined.
4. **Add Sweeteners and Flavorings:**
   - Stir in the piloncillo (or sugar), cocoa powder, ground cinnamon (if using), and a pinch of salt. If using a Mexican chocolate tablet, grate it or chop it finely and add it to the mixture for extra richness and flavor. Stir continuously over medium heat until the champurrado thickens slightly and reaches your desired consistency. This usually takes about 10-15 minutes.
5. **Adjust Consistency and Flavor:**
   - If the champurrado is too thick, you can add more water or milk to thin it out. If it's too thin, continue cooking until it thickens to your liking. Taste and adjust sweetness or add a splash of vanilla extract if desired.
6. **Serve Hot:**
   - Ladle the champurrado into mugs or cups. Serve hot, optionally topped with whipped cream and a sprinkle of ground cinnamon or cocoa powder on top for garnish.

Tips:

- **Variations:** Some recipes include adding almond extract or anise seeds for additional flavor nuances. Adjust the spices and sweetness levels to suit your taste preferences.
- **Storage:** Champurrado is best enjoyed fresh but can be stored in the refrigerator for up to 2 days. Reheat gently on the stove or in the microwave before serving.

Champurrado is a comforting and indulgent beverage that captures the essence of Mexican flavors. Whether you enjoy it on its own or paired with traditional Mexican pastries like pan dulce, it's sure to warm both body and soul.

Pan de Elote (Cornbread)

Ingredients:

- 4 cups fresh corn kernels (about 4-5 ears of corn)
- 1 cup all-purpose flour
- 1 cup sugar (adjust to taste)
- 1/2 cup milk
- 1/2 cup unsalted butter, melted
- 3 eggs
- 1 teaspoon baking powder
- 1 teaspoon vanilla extract
- Pinch of salt

Instructions:

1. **Preheat** your oven to 350°F (175°C). Grease and flour a baking dish or line it with parchment paper.
2. **Blend** the corn kernels in a blender or food processor until smooth. You can leave it a bit chunky if you prefer some texture.
3. In a large bowl, **combine** the blended corn, melted butter, milk, sugar, eggs, vanilla extract, and salt. Mix well until everything is thoroughly incorporated.
4. **Sift** in the flour and baking powder. Stir gently until the dry ingredients are just combined with the wet ingredients. Be careful not to overmix; a few lumps are okay.
5. Pour the batter into the prepared baking dish, spreading it out evenly.
6. **Bake** in the preheated oven for about 45-55 minutes, or until a toothpick inserted into the center comes out clean.
7. Once baked, **remove** from the oven and let it cool in the pan for about 10 minutes. Then, transfer to a wire rack to cool completely before slicing and serving.

Serving Suggestions:

- Serve pan de elote warm or at room temperature.
- It pairs wonderfully with a hot cup of coffee or Mexican hot chocolate.
- You can dust it with powdered sugar or serve it with a dollop of whipped cream or vanilla ice cream for a delightful dessert.

Enjoy this delicious and comforting Mexican treat that celebrates the natural sweetness of corn!

Tacos de Pescado (Fish Tacos)

Ingredients:

For the fish:

- 1 lb (450g) firm white fish fillets (such as cod, tilapia, or mahi-mahi)
- 1/2 cup all-purpose flour
- 1/2 teaspoon salt
- 1/2 teaspoon ground cumin
- 1/2 teaspoon smoked paprika
- 1/4 teaspoon black pepper
- Vegetable oil, for frying

For the cabbage slaw:

- 2 cups shredded cabbage (green or purple, or a mix)
- 1/4 cup chopped fresh cilantro
- 1/4 cup mayonnaise
- 1 tablespoon lime juice
- Salt and pepper, to taste

For assembling:

- Corn tortillas (8-10)
- Sliced avocado
- Sliced radishes (optional)
- Lime wedges
- Hot sauce or salsa (optional)

Instructions:

1. **Prepare the fish:**
    - Cut the fish fillets into strips, about 1 inch wide.
    - In a shallow bowl, combine the flour, salt, cumin, paprika, and black pepper.
    - Heat about 1/4 inch of vegetable oil in a large skillet over medium-high heat.
    - Dredge each fish strip in the flour mixture, shaking off excess, and place them in the hot oil. Cook for 3-4 minutes per side, or until golden brown and cooked through. Remove to a paper towel-lined plate to drain excess oil.
2. **Make the cabbage slaw:**
    - In a bowl, combine the shredded cabbage, chopped cilantro, mayonnaise, lime juice, salt, and pepper. Toss until well coated. Adjust seasoning to taste.
3. **Warm the tortillas:**
    - Heat the corn tortillas on a dry skillet over medium heat for about 30 seconds per side, until warm and pliable. Alternatively, you can wrap them in a damp paper towel and microwave for 20-30 seconds.
4. **Assemble the tacos:**

- Place a few pieces of fried fish onto each tortilla.
- Top with a generous spoonful of the cabbage slaw.
- Add slices of avocado and radishes, if using.
- Squeeze fresh lime juice over the top and drizzle with hot sauce or salsa, if desired.
5. **Serve immediately**, with extra lime wedges and hot sauce on the side.

Tips:

- **Variations:** You can customize your fish tacos by using different types of fish or adding additional toppings like diced tomatoes, pickled onions, or cotija cheese.
- **Corn Tortillas:** Corn tortillas are traditional for fish tacos, but you can use flour tortillas if you prefer.
- **Sides:** Serve with rice and beans, Mexican street corn (elote), or a side of chips and salsa.

Enjoy these flavorful fish tacos that bring together crispy fish, creamy slaw, and fresh toppings for a delicious and satisfying meal!

Barbacoa

Ingredients:

- 3 lbs (1.5 kg) beef chuck roast or brisket, cut into large chunks
- 4 cloves garlic, minced
- 2 chipotle peppers in adobo sauce, chopped (adjust to taste)
- 1 small onion, chopped
- 1/4 cup fresh lime juice
- 1/4 cup apple cider vinegar
- 3 bay leaves
- 1 tablespoon ground cumin
- 1 tablespoon dried oregano
- 1 teaspoon ground cloves
- 1 teaspoon ground cinnamon
- 1 teaspoon salt, or to taste
- 1/2 teaspoon black pepper
- 1/2 cup beef broth or water

Optional toppings and sides:

- Chopped fresh cilantro
- Diced onion
- Lime wedges
- Salsa or pico de gallo
- Warm corn or flour tortillas
- Rice and beans

Instructions:

1. **Prepare the marinade:** In a blender or food processor, combine the minced garlic, chopped chipotle peppers, chopped onion, lime juice, apple cider vinegar, bay leaves, cumin, oregano, cloves, cinnamon, salt, and black pepper. Blend until smooth.
2. **Marinate the meat:** Place the beef chunks in a large bowl or resealable plastic bag. Pour the marinade over the meat, making sure all pieces are well coated. Cover or seal and refrigerate for at least 2 hours, preferably overnight.
3. **Slow cook the barbacoa:**
   - Transfer the marinated meat and marinade to a slow cooker. Add the beef broth or water.
   - Cover and cook on low for 8-10 hours, or until the meat is very tender and easily shreds with a fork.
4. **Shred the meat:** Once cooked, remove the meat from the slow cooker and shred it using two forks. Remove any excess fat.
5. **Serve:** Serve the shredded barbacoa in warm tortillas with your choice of toppings such as chopped cilantro, diced onion, salsa, and a squeeze of fresh lime juice. It's also great with rice and beans on the side.

Notes:

- **Adjusting spice level:** If you prefer a spicier barbacoa, you can add more chipotle peppers or include some of the adobo sauce from the can.
- **Storage:** Leftover barbacoa can be stored in an airtight container in the refrigerator for 3-4 days or frozen for up to 3 months. Reheat gently in a skillet or microwave.

Enjoy the rich, savory flavors of homemade barbacoa, perfect for tacos, burritos, nachos, or simply served over rice for a satisfying meal!

Horchata

Ingredients:

- 1 cup long-grain white rice
- 2 cinnamon sticks

- 4 cups water, divided
- 1/2 cup milk (optional, for a creamier horchata)
- 1/2 cup granulated sugar (adjust to taste)
- 1 teaspoon vanilla extract
- Ground cinnamon, for garnish

Instructions:

1. **Rinse the rice:** Rinse the rice under cold water until the water runs clear. This helps remove excess starch.
2. **Soak the rice and cinnamon:** In a blender, combine the rinsed rice and cinnamon sticks with 2 cups of water. Blend on high speed until the rice and cinnamon sticks are roughly ground, about 1 minute.
3. **Let it soak:** Transfer the rice mixture to a bowl and add another 2 cups of water. Cover and let it soak at room temperature for at least 3 hours or overnight in the refrigerator. This soaking process helps soften the rice and infuse the water with flavor.
4. **Blend and strain:** After soaking, blend the rice mixture again until it forms a smooth paste, about 1-2 minutes. Add the milk (if using), sugar, and vanilla extract. Blend until well combined.
5. **Strain the mixture:** Place a fine-mesh sieve, cheesecloth, or a nut milk bag over a pitcher or bowl. Pour the blended mixture through the sieve to strain out the rice solids. Use a spoon to press down on the solids to extract as much liquid as possible. Discard the rice solids or save them for other recipes.
6. **Chill and serve:** Once strained, refrigerate the horchata until cold, about 1-2 hours. Stir well before serving. Serve over ice and sprinkle ground cinnamon on top for garnish, if desired.
7. **Enjoy:** Horchata is best served chilled. It's a perfect accompaniment to spicy foods or enjoyed on its own as a refreshing drink.

Notes:

- **Variations:** Some regions in Mexico make horchata with almonds or other nuts. You can experiment by adding a handful of blanched almonds or other nuts to the soaking mixture for a different flavor.
- **Storage:** Horchata can be stored in the refrigerator for up to 3-4 days. Stir well before serving if it separates.

This homemade horchata recipe captures the essence of this beloved Mexican beverage, perfect for cooling down on a hot day or enjoying alongside your favorite Mexican dishes.

Tamale Pie

Ingredients:

For the cornbread crust:

- 1 cup cornmeal
- 1 cup all-purpose flour

- 1 tablespoon baking powder
- 1/2 teaspoon salt
- 1/4 cup granulated sugar
- 1 cup milk
- 1/4 cup vegetable oil
- 1 egg

For the filling:

- 1 tablespoon vegetable oil
- 1 onion, chopped
- 2 cloves garlic, minced
- 1 red bell pepper, chopped
- 1 lb (450g) ground beef or turkey
- 1 tablespoon chili powder
- 1 teaspoon ground cumin
- 1/2 teaspoon dried oregano
- 1/2 teaspoon salt, or to taste
- 1/4 teaspoon black pepper
- 1 can (14.5 oz) diced tomatoes, drained
- 1 can (4 oz) diced green chilies
- 1 cup frozen corn kernels
- 1 cup shredded cheddar cheese (or Mexican blend cheese)

Instructions:

1. **Preheat** your oven to 400°F (200°C). Grease a 9x13 inch baking dish.
2. **Make the cornbread crust:**
   - In a large bowl, whisk together the cornmeal, flour, baking powder, salt, and sugar.
   - In another bowl, whisk together the milk, vegetable oil, and egg.
   - Pour the wet ingredients into the dry ingredients and stir until just combined. Set aside.
3. **Prepare the filling:**
   - Heat the vegetable oil in a large skillet over medium heat. Add the chopped onion, garlic, and red bell pepper. Cook until softened, about 5 minutes.
   - Add the ground beef or turkey to the skillet. Cook, breaking up the meat with a spoon, until browned and cooked through.
   - Stir in the chili powder, cumin, oregano, salt, and black pepper. Cook for another minute until fragrant.
   - Add the drained diced tomatoes, diced green chilies, and frozen corn kernels. Stir to combine. Remove from heat.
4. **Assemble the tamale pie:**
   - Spread the meat and vegetable mixture evenly into the prepared baking dish.
   - Sprinkle the shredded cheese evenly over the filling.

- Pour the cornbread batter over the top, spreading it out to cover the filling completely.
5. **Bake the tamale pie:**
   - Place the baking dish in the preheated oven and bake for 25-30 minutes, or until the cornbread crust is golden brown and cooked through.
6. **Serve:** Remove from the oven and let it cool for a few minutes before serving. Cut into squares and serve hot.

Tips:

- **Variations:** You can customize the filling by adding black beans, diced jalapeños for extra spice, or different types of cheese.
- **Make it vegetarian:** Substitute the ground meat with cooked lentils or additional vegetables for a vegetarian version.
- **Serving suggestion:** Serve tamale pie with sour cream, guacamole, or salsa on the side for added flavor.

This tamale pie recipe is a comforting and hearty dish that brings together the flavors of cornbread and savory filling, reminiscent of traditional tamales but easier to make in casserole form.

Tostadas de Tinga

Ingredients:

For the tinga:

- 1 lb (450g) boneless, skinless chicken breasts or thighs
- 1 onion, chopped
- 2 cloves garlic, minced

- 1 can (14.5 oz) diced tomatoes
- 2-3 chipotle peppers in adobo sauce, chopped (adjust to taste)
- 1 teaspoon dried oregano
- 1/2 teaspoon ground cumin
- Salt and pepper, to taste
- 1 tablespoon vegetable oil

For the tostadas:

- Corn tostada shells (store-bought or homemade)
- Refried beans (optional)
- Shredded lettuce
- Diced tomatoes
- Sliced avocado or guacamole
- Crumbled queso fresco or shredded cheese
- Chopped fresh cilantro
- Lime wedges

Instructions:

1. **Prepare the tinga:**
    - In a large pot or Dutch oven, heat the vegetable oil over medium-high heat. Add the chopped onion and cook until softened, about 5 minutes.
    - Add the minced garlic and cook for another minute until fragrant.
    - Add the diced tomatoes (with their juices), chopped chipotle peppers, dried oregano, ground cumin, salt, and pepper. Stir to combine.
    - Add the chicken breasts or thighs to the pot, making sure they are submerged in the sauce.
    - Bring the mixture to a boil, then reduce the heat to low, cover, and simmer for about 20-25 minutes, or until the chicken is cooked through and tender.
    - Remove the chicken from the pot and shred it using two forks. Return the shredded chicken to the pot and stir to coat it evenly with the tinga sauce. Simmer for another 5-10 minutes to allow the flavors to meld together.
2. **Assemble the tostadas:**
    - If using, spread a thin layer of refried beans on each tostada shell.
    - Top each tostada with a generous portion of the tinga chicken mixture.
    - Add shredded lettuce, diced tomatoes, sliced avocado or guacamole, and crumbled queso fresco or shredded cheese on top of the chicken.
    - Garnish with chopped fresh cilantro and serve with lime wedges on the side.
3. **Serve immediately**, allowing everyone to squeeze lime juice over their tostadas before enjoying.

Tips:

- **Adjusting spice level:** If you prefer spicier tinga, you can add more chopped chipotle peppers or some of the adobo sauce from the can.
- **Make it ahead:** Tinga can be made ahead of time and stored in the refrigerator for up to 3 days. Reheat gently before serving.
- **Variations:** You can also use pork (such as pork shoulder) or beef (such as brisket) instead of chicken for different variations of tinga.

Tostadas de tinga are perfect for a casual dinner or as a party appetizer. They offer a delightful mix of flavors and textures that are sure to be a hit with your family and friends!

Caldo de Res (Beef Soup)

Ingredients:

- 2 lbs (about 1 kg) beef shank or beef chuck roast, bone-in, cut into large chunks
- 8 cups beef broth or water
- 1 onion, chopped

- 3 cloves garlic, minced
- 2 tomatoes, chopped
- 2 carrots, peeled and sliced into rounds
- 2 potatoes, peeled and cut into chunks
- 2 ears of corn, husked and cut into thirds (or 1 cup frozen corn kernels)
- 1 zucchini, sliced into rounds or chunks
- 2 chayotes, peeled, seeded, and cut into chunks (optional)
- 2 tablespoons chopped fresh cilantro
- 1 teaspoon dried oregano
- 1 bay leaf
- Salt and pepper, to taste
- Lime wedges, for serving
- Warm corn tortillas, for serving

Instructions:

1. **Prepare the beef:**
   - In a large pot, combine the beef chunks with the beef broth or water. Bring to a boil over medium-high heat, then reduce the heat to low and simmer, covered, for about 1 hour. Skim off any foam that rises to the surface.
2. **Add aromatics and vegetables:**
   - Add the chopped onion, minced garlic, chopped tomatoes, dried oregano, bay leaf, salt, and pepper to the pot. Stir to combine.
3. **Continue cooking:**
   - Simmer the soup for another 30 minutes, or until the beef is tender.
4. **Add vegetables:**
   - Add the sliced carrots, potatoes, corn pieces (if using fresh), and chayotes (if using). Simmer for 15-20 minutes, or until the vegetables are tender.
5. **Add zucchini and corn (if using frozen):**
   - Add the zucchini slices and frozen corn kernels (if using). Simmer for another 5-10 minutes, until the zucchini is tender.
6. **Adjust seasoning:**
   - Taste the soup and adjust seasoning with more salt and pepper if needed. Stir in the chopped cilantro.
7. **Serve:**
   - Ladle the caldo de res into bowls, making sure to include beef, vegetables, and broth in each serving. Serve hot with lime wedges on the side and warm corn tortillas.

Tips:

- **Variations:** You can customize your caldo de res by adding other vegetables such as green beans, cabbage, or celery.

- **Storage:** Caldo de res can be stored in the refrigerator for up to 3-4 days. The flavors often improve the next day as the ingredients meld together.
- **Garnish:** Garnish with additional chopped cilantro or diced onion for extra flavor.

Caldo de res is a wholesome and nutritious soup that's perfect for warming up on chilly days. It's a complete meal in itself, packed with tender beef, a variety of vegetables, and a rich broth that's both comforting and satisfying.

Jicama Salad

Ingredients:

- 1 medium jicama, peeled and julienned or sliced into matchsticks
- 1 large cucumber, peeled and sliced into thin rounds or half-moons
- 1 orange, peeled and segmented

- 1/4 cup fresh lime juice (about 2-3 limes)
- 2 tablespoons olive oil
- 1 teaspoon honey or agave syrup (optional, for sweetness)
- 1/2 teaspoon chili powder (adjust to taste)
- Salt and pepper, to taste
- Fresh cilantro leaves, chopped (optional, for garnish)

Instructions:

1. **Prepare the jicama and cucumber:**
   - Peel the jicama using a vegetable peeler. Cut it into thin matchsticks or slices. Place in a large bowl.
   - Peel the cucumber and cut it into thin rounds or half-moons. Add to the bowl with the jicama.
2. **Prepare the orange:**
   - Peel the orange and cut it into segments. Remove any seeds. Add the orange segments to the bowl with the jicama and cucumber.
3. **Make the dressing:**
   - In a small bowl, whisk together the fresh lime juice, olive oil, honey or agave syrup (if using), chili powder, salt, and pepper. Adjust seasoning to taste.
4. **Assemble the salad:**
   - Pour the dressing over the jicama, cucumber, and orange in the bowl. Gently toss to combine, ensuring the salad is evenly coated with the dressing.
5. **Chill and serve:**
   - Cover the bowl and refrigerate the salad for at least 30 minutes to allow the flavors to meld together.
6. **Garnish and serve:**
   - Before serving, taste and adjust seasoning if needed. Sprinkle chopped fresh cilantro leaves on top for garnish, if desired.
7. **Enjoy:** Serve the jicama salad chilled as a refreshing side dish or light appetizer.

Tips:

- **Variations:** You can add other ingredients to your jicama salad, such as diced avocado, sliced radishes, or red onion for additional flavor and crunch.
- **Storage:** Jicama salad is best enjoyed fresh but can be stored in an airtight container in the refrigerator for up to 2 days. The flavors may intensify as it sits.

This jicama salad recipe highlights the natural crispness and sweetness of jicama, complemented by citrusy tang and a touch of spice, making it a perfect dish for summer gatherings or as a refreshing side to complement a variety of meals.

Alambre

Ingredients:

- 1 lb (450g) beef sirloin or skirt steak, thinly sliced
- 1 onion, thinly sliced
- 1 red bell pepper, thinly sliced
- 1 green bell pepper, thinly sliced

- 4 slices of bacon, chopped
- 1 tablespoon vegetable oil
- 1 tablespoon soy sauce
- 1 tablespoon Worcestershire sauce
- 1 tablespoon fresh lime juice
- 1 teaspoon ground cumin
- Salt and pepper, to taste
- Fresh cilantro, chopped (for garnish)
- Lime wedges, for serving
- Warm corn or flour tortillas, for serving

Instructions:

1. **Prepare the marinade:**
   - In a bowl, combine the soy sauce, Worcestershire sauce, lime juice, ground cumin, salt, and pepper. Mix well.
2. **Marinate the meat:**
   - Place the thinly sliced beef in a bowl and pour the marinade over it. Toss to coat the meat evenly. Let it marinate for at least 30 minutes in the refrigerator.
3. **Cook the bacon and vegetables:**
   - In a large skillet or frying pan, heat the vegetable oil over medium heat. Add the chopped bacon and cook until it starts to brown and crisp up.
   - Add the sliced onion and bell peppers to the skillet with the bacon. Cook, stirring occasionally, until the vegetables are softened and slightly caramelized, about 5-7 minutes. Remove from the skillet and set aside.
4. **Cook the marinated meat:**
   - In the same skillet or a grill pan over medium-high heat, add the marinated beef slices in a single layer (you may need to do this in batches). Cook for 2-3 minutes per side, or until the meat is cooked through and nicely browned. Remove from the skillet and set aside.
5. **Assemble the alambre:**
   - Return the cooked vegetables and bacon to the skillet. Add the cooked beef slices back into the skillet. Stir everything together and cook for another minute or two, allowing the flavors to meld together.
6. **Serve:**
   - Transfer the alambre mixture to a serving dish. Garnish with chopped fresh cilantro. Serve hot with warm tortillas and lime wedges on the side.

Tips:

- **Variations:** You can customize your alambre by adding different vegetables such as mushrooms, tomatoes, or even pineapple for a sweet twist.
- **Serving suggestions:** Serve alambre with refried beans, guacamole, salsa, or a side of Mexican rice for a complete meal.

- **Leftovers:** Alambre leftovers can be stored in an airtight container in the refrigerator for up to 3 days. Reheat gently in a skillet or microwave before serving.

Enjoy this flavorful and satisfying Mexican dish of alambre, perfect for a casual dinner or for entertaining friends and family!

Gorditas

Ingredients:

For the gorditas:

- 2 cups masa harina (corn flour for tortillas)
- 1/2 teaspoon salt
- 1 1/4 cups warm water
- Vegetable oil, for frying

For the filling (choose one or more):

- Shredded beef or chicken tinga
- Refried beans
- Picadillo (ground beef with potatoes and carrots)
- Chorizo with potatoes
- Rajas con crema (strips of roasted poblano peppers in cream sauce)
- Cheese (queso fresco, shredded cheese, or melted cheese)

Optional toppings:

- Shredded lettuce
- Diced tomatoes
- Sliced avocado or guacamole
- Salsa (red or green)
- Crema (Mexican sour cream)
- Chopped fresh cilantro
- Lime wedges

Instructions:

1. **Prepare the masa dough:**
   - In a large bowl, combine the masa harina and salt. Gradually add the warm water, mixing with your hands, until a soft dough forms. The dough should be firm and not sticky. If it feels dry, add a little more water; if too wet, add a bit more masa harina.
2. **Shape the gorditas:**
   - Divide the masa dough into golf ball-sized portions. Roll each portion into a ball, then flatten it into a disk about 1/2 inch thick and 3-4 inches in diameter. You can use your hands or a tortilla press lined with plastic wrap.
3. **Cook the gorditas:**
   - Heat a skillet or griddle over medium-high heat. Lightly grease the surface with vegetable oil.
   - Cook each gordita for about 2-3 minutes on each side, or until golden brown and slightly puffed. Press down gently with a spatula as they cook to ensure even browning.
4. **Create a pocket:**
   - While the gorditas are still warm, carefully make a slit along one edge to create a pocket. Be careful not to cut all the way through.
5. **Fill the gorditas:**
   - Fill each gordita with your choice of filling(s) and toppings. You can mix and match fillings according to your preference.
6. **Serve:**
   - Serve gorditas warm, topped with additional toppings if desired. They are often enjoyed as a handheld snack or light meal.

Tips:

- **Variations:** Gorditas can be filled with a wide range of savory fillings, making them versatile. Experiment with different combinations to find your favorite.
- **Storage:** Store any leftover gorditas (unfilled) in an airtight container at room temperature for up to 2 days. Reheat in a skillet or toaster oven before filling and serving.
- **Authentic toppings:** For an authentic touch, consider topping your gorditas with traditional Mexican ingredients like crumbled queso fresco, chopped cilantro, and a squeeze of fresh lime juice.

Enjoy making and savoring these homemade gorditas, a beloved dish that showcases the rich flavors and textures of Mexican cuisine!

Cochinita Pibil

Ingredients:

For the marinade:

- 3-4 lbs (1.5-2 kg) pork shoulder or pork butt, cut into large chunks
- 3-4 tablespoons annatto paste (achiote paste)
- 1/2 cup orange juice (preferably fresh)
- 1/4 cup lime juice (preferably fresh)
- 4 cloves garlic, minced
- 1 teaspoon ground cumin

- 1 teaspoon dried oregano
- 1/2 teaspoon ground cinnamon
- 1/2 teaspoon ground cloves
- Salt and pepper, to taste

For cooking:

- Banana leaves or aluminum foil (if banana leaves are not available)
- 1 red onion, thinly sliced
- 2-3 bay leaves
- 1/2 cup chicken broth or water
- Vegetable oil, for greasing

To serve:

- Corn tortillas
- Pickled red onions (optional)
- Fresh cilantro, chopped
- Lime wedges

Instructions:

1. **Prepare the marinade:**
    - In a bowl, combine the annatto paste, orange juice, lime juice, minced garlic, ground cumin, dried oregano, ground cinnamon, ground cloves, salt, and pepper. Mix well until the annatto paste is dissolved and the marinade is well combined.
2. **Marinate the pork:**
    - Place the pork chunks in a large bowl or resealable plastic bag. Pour the marinade over the pork, ensuring all pieces are well coated. Marinate in the refrigerator for at least 4 hours, preferably overnight, to allow the flavors to penetrate the meat.
3. **Prepare for cooking:**
    - Preheat your oven to 325°F (160°C).
    - If using banana leaves: briefly pass them over a flame to soften and make them pliable. This step helps release their natural oils and enhances flavor. Cut them into pieces large enough to wrap the pork.
4. **Assemble and cook:**
    - Grease a baking dish with vegetable oil. Line the dish with banana leaves or aluminum foil.
    - Arrange the marinated pork chunks in the baking dish. Top with thinly sliced red onion and bay leaves. Pour the chicken broth or water over the pork.
    - Wrap the pork tightly with banana leaves or aluminum foil, ensuring it's well-sealed to trap steam and flavors.
5. **Bake:** Place the baking dish in the preheated oven and bake for 3-4 hours, or until the pork is very tender and pulls apart easily with a fork.

6. **Serve:**
   - Once cooked, shred the pork using two forks. Serve Cochinita Pibil warm, wrapped in warm corn tortillas.
   - Garnish with pickled red onions, fresh cilantro, and lime wedges on the side for squeezing over the tacos.

Tips:

- **Annatto paste substitute:** If you can't find annatto paste, you can make a substitute by mixing annatto seeds (achiote seeds) with vinegar or citrus juice until it forms a paste-like consistency.
- **Authenticity:** For a more authentic touch, consider using banana leaves for wrapping the pork. They impart a unique flavor and help keep the pork moist during cooking.
- **Leftovers:** Cochinita Pibil freezes well. Store cooled leftovers in an airtight container in the freezer for up to 2-3 months. Thaw overnight in the refrigerator before reheating gently on the stove or in the microwave.

Enjoy this flavorful and aromatic dish of Cochinita Pibil, perfect for sharing with family and friends, and savor the rich flavors of Yucatecan cuisine!

Birria de Res

Ingredients:

For the Birria:

- 3 lbs (about 1.5 kg) beef chuck roast or brisket, cut into large chunks
- 1 onion, chopped
- 4 cloves garlic, minced
- 2 bay leaves
- 2 teaspoons ground cumin
- 1 teaspoon dried oregano

- 1 teaspoon smoked paprika (optional, for added smokiness)
- 1/2 teaspoon ground cloves
- 1/2 teaspoon ground cinnamon
- 2-3 dried guajillo chilies, stemmed and seeded
- 2-3 dried ancho chilies, stemmed and seeded
- 4 cups beef broth (or water)
- 1/2 cup apple cider vinegar (or white vinegar)
- Salt and pepper, to taste
- Vegetable oil, for cooking

For serving:

- Corn tortillas
- Chopped onion and cilantro, for garnish
- Lime wedges
- Salsa (optional)

Instructions:

1. **Prepare the Chilies:**
   - In a dry skillet over medium heat, toast the dried guajillo and ancho chilies for about 1-2 minutes per side until they become fragrant. Remove from heat and let them cool slightly.
   - Once cooled, transfer the toasted chilies to a bowl and cover with hot water. Let them soak for about 15-20 minutes until softened.
2. **Make the Birria Sauce:**
   - In a blender or food processor, combine the softened chilies (drained from soaking water), chopped onion, minced garlic, ground cumin, dried oregano, smoked paprika (if using), ground cloves, ground cinnamon, and 1 cup of beef broth. Blend until smooth, adding more broth if needed to achieve a smooth consistency.
3. **Cook the Birria:**
   - Season the beef chunks with salt and pepper.
   - In a large Dutch oven or heavy-bottomed pot, heat a tablespoon of vegetable oil over medium-high heat. Brown the beef chunks in batches, about 3-4 minutes per side, until nicely browned. Remove and set aside.
   - In the same pot, add a bit more oil if needed and sauté the chopped onion until translucent, about 5 minutes. Add the minced garlic and cook for another minute until fragrant.
   - Return the browned beef chunks to the pot. Pour the birria sauce over the meat.
   - Add the remaining beef broth and apple cider vinegar. Stir to combine. Bring to a boil, then reduce the heat to low. Cover and simmer gently for 2.5 to 3 hours, or until the beef is tender and can be easily shredded with a fork.
4. **Serve Birria de Res:**
   - Once the beef is tender, remove it from the pot and shred it using two forks.

- Skim any excess fat from the surface of the broth. Taste and adjust seasoning with salt and pepper if needed.
- Serve Birria de Res warm in bowls, garnished with chopped onion, cilantro, and a squeeze of lime juice. Serve with warm corn tortillas on the side for dipping or making tacos.

5. **Consommé (Optional):**
    - If desired, strain the cooking liquid to serve as consommé alongside the Birria. This flavorful broth can be used for dipping tacos or served as a soup.

Tips:

- **Variations:** You can adjust the spiciness of Birria de Res by adding more or fewer dried chilies. You can also add a couple of chipotle peppers in adobo sauce for a smoky kick.
- **Storage:** Birria de Res freezes well. Store cooled leftovers in an airtight container in the refrigerator for up to 3 days, or freeze for up to 2-3 months.
- **Traditional serving:** Serve Birria de Res with chopped onion and cilantro, lime wedges, and warm corn tortillas. Optionally, offer salsa on the side for those who enjoy an extra kick.

Enjoy making and savoring this rich and flavorful Mexican dish of Birria de Res!

Chiles en Nogada

Ingredients:

For the picadillo:

- 1 lb (450g) ground beef or pork
- 2 tablespoons vegetable oil
- 1 onion, finely chopped
- 2 cloves garlic, minced
- 2 tomatoes, chopped

- 1/4 cup raisins
- 1/4 cup slivered almonds
- 1/4 cup chopped walnuts
- 1/4 cup diced apple
- 1/4 cup diced pear
- 1 plantain or banana, diced
- 1/2 teaspoon ground cinnamon
- 1/4 teaspoon ground cloves
- 1/4 teaspoon ground nutmeg
- Salt and pepper, to taste

For the walnut sauce (nogada):

- 1 cup walnuts, shelled and chopped
- 1 cup milk
- 1/2 cup Mexican crema or sour cream
- 1/4 cup queso fresco or mild cheese, crumbled
- 1 tablespoon sugar
- 1/4 teaspoon ground cinnamon
- Salt, to taste

For assembling:

- 6-8 poblano chilies, roasted, peeled, and seeded
- Pomegranate seeds, for garnish
- Fresh parsley, chopped, for garnish

Instructions:

1. **Prepare the picadillo:**
    - In a large skillet, heat the vegetable oil over medium heat. Add the chopped onion and minced garlic. Cook until softened, about 5 minutes.
    - Add the ground meat and cook until browned, breaking it up with a spoon as it cooks.
    - Stir in the chopped tomatoes, raisins, slivered almonds, chopped walnuts, diced apple, diced pear, and diced plantain or banana.
    - Season with ground cinnamon, ground cloves, ground nutmeg, salt, and pepper. Cook for another 10-15 minutes, stirring occasionally, until the flavors meld together and the picadillo is cooked through. Remove from heat and set aside.
2. **Prepare the walnut sauce (nogada):**
    - In a blender or food processor, combine the chopped walnuts, milk, Mexican crema or sour cream, crumbled queso fresco or mild cheese, sugar, ground cinnamon, and a pinch of salt. Blend until smooth and creamy. Adjust seasoning to taste. If the sauce is too thick, you can add a little more milk to achieve a pourable consistency.

3. **Assemble the Chiles en Nogada:**
    - Carefully stuff each roasted poblano chili with the prepared picadillo mixture. Be gentle to avoid tearing the chilies.
    - Place the stuffed chilies on a serving platter or individual plates.
    - Pour the walnut sauce (nogada) generously over the stuffed chilies.
4. **Garnish and serve:**
    - Sprinkle pomegranate seeds generously over the walnut sauce.
    - Garnish with chopped fresh parsley for a pop of color.
    - Serve Chiles en Nogada immediately, while the walnut sauce is still warm.

Tips:

- **Roasting poblano chilies:** You can roast poblano chilies over an open flame, on a grill, or under a broiler until the skin is charred and blistered. Let them steam in a covered bowl for a few minutes, then peel off the skin and remove the seeds.
- **Make-ahead:** You can prepare the picadillo and walnut sauce (nogada) ahead of time. Store them separately in the refrigerator and assemble just before serving.
- **Presentation:** Chiles en Nogada are traditionally served at room temperature or slightly warm. They are a beautiful dish with vibrant colors that make them perfect for special occasions.

Enjoy preparing and savoring Chiles en Nogada, a dish that embodies the flavors and colors of Mexican cuisine and culture!

Mexican Rice

Ingredients:

- 1 cup long-grain white rice
- 1 tablespoon vegetable oil or olive oil
- 1 small onion, finely chopped
- 2 cloves garlic, minced
- 1 tomato, chopped
- 1 tablespoon tomato paste
- 1 3/4 cups chicken broth (or vegetable broth for a vegetarian version)

- 1 teaspoon ground cumin
- 1/2 teaspoon chili powder (adjust to taste)
- Salt and pepper, to taste
- Fresh cilantro, chopped (optional, for garnish)
- Lime wedges (optional, for serving)

Instructions:

1. **Rinse and prepare the rice:**
   - Rinse the rice under cold water until the water runs clear. This helps remove excess starch and prevents the rice from becoming sticky when cooked.
2. **Sauté the aromatics:**
   - In a large skillet or saucepan, heat the vegetable oil over medium heat. Add the chopped onion and cook for 3-4 minutes, until softened and translucent.
   - Add the minced garlic and cook for another 1-2 minutes, until fragrant.
3. **Toast the rice:**
   - Add the rinsed rice to the skillet with the onion and garlic. Stir frequently and cook for 2-3 minutes, allowing the rice to toast slightly. This step adds flavor and helps keep the rice grains separate when cooked.
4. **Add tomatoes and spices:**
   - Stir in the chopped tomato and tomato paste. Cook for another 2-3 minutes, until the tomatoes begin to break down and release their juices.
   - Add the ground cumin, chili powder, salt, and pepper to the skillet. Stir well to combine and coat the rice evenly with the spices.
5. **Cook the rice:**
   - Pour the chicken broth (or vegetable broth) into the skillet, stirring to combine everything well. Bring the mixture to a boil.
   - Reduce the heat to low, cover the skillet with a lid, and simmer for 15-20 minutes, or until the rice is tender and has absorbed all the liquid. Avoid stirring the rice during cooking to prevent it from becoming sticky.
6. **Fluff and serve:**
   - Once the rice is cooked, remove the skillet from the heat. Let it sit, covered, for a few minutes.
   - Fluff the Mexican rice with a fork to separate the grains. Taste and adjust seasoning with more salt and pepper if needed.
7. **Garnish and serve:**
   - Transfer the Mexican rice to a serving dish. Garnish with chopped fresh cilantro, if desired.
   - Serve hot, accompanied by lime wedges for squeezing over the rice.

Tips:

- **Variations:** You can add diced bell peppers, corn kernels, or peas to the rice for added texture and flavor.

- **Storage:** Mexican rice can be stored in an airtight container in the refrigerator for up to 3-4 days. Reheat gently in the microwave or on the stovetop with a splash of broth or water to refresh.
- **Serve with:** Mexican rice pairs well with a variety of dishes such as tacos, enchiladas, burritos, or grilled meats.

Enjoy making this classic Mexican rice recipe at home, perfect for bringing vibrant flavors to your table!

Polvorones (Mexican Wedding Cookies)

Ingredients:

- 1 cup (2 sticks) unsalted butter, softened
- 1/2 cup powdered sugar, plus extra for coating
- 1 teaspoon vanilla extract
- 2 cups all-purpose flour
- 1/4 teaspoon salt
- 1 cup finely chopped pecans or walnuts (optional)

Instructions:

1. **Preheat oven and prepare baking sheet:**
   - Preheat your oven to 350°F (175°C). Line a baking sheet with parchment paper or silicone baking mat.
2. **Cream butter and sugar:**
   - In a mixing bowl, beat the softened butter until creamy using a hand mixer or stand mixer with a paddle attachment.
   - Add 1/2 cup powdered sugar and vanilla extract to the butter. Continue beating until light and fluffy.
3. **Mix dry ingredients:**
   - In a separate bowl, whisk together the flour and salt.
4. **Combine wet and dry ingredients:**
   - Gradually add the flour mixture to the butter mixture, mixing on low speed until just combined. Be careful not to overmix.
5. **Add nuts (if using):**
   - Fold in the finely chopped pecans or walnuts until evenly distributed in the dough. This step is optional but adds a nice crunch to the cookies.
6. **Shape the cookies:**
   - Take about 1 tablespoon of dough and roll it into a ball (or you can shape them into crescents or small rounds). Place the shaped cookies onto the prepared baking sheet, spacing them about 1 inch apart.
7. **Bake:**
   - Bake the cookies in the preheated oven for 12-15 minutes, or until the bottoms are lightly golden. The tops should still be pale.
8. **Cool and coat:**
   - Allow the cookies to cool on the baking sheet for a few minutes, then transfer them to a wire rack to cool completely.
   - Once cooled, roll each cookie in powdered sugar until fully coated. You can also dust them lightly with powdered sugar using a sifter.
9. **Serve or store:**
   - Arrange the Polvorones on a serving platter and enjoy! They can be stored in an airtight container at room temperature for several days.

Tips:

- **Variations:** You can customize these cookies by adding a pinch of cinnamon or nutmeg to the dough for a spiced flavor.
- **Nuts:** If you prefer, you can omit the nuts altogether or use a different type of nuts such as almonds or pistachios.
- **Powdered sugar coating:** For a thicker coating of powdered sugar, you can roll the cookies in powdered sugar twice, letting them cool completely between coatings.

These Polvorones are perfect for celebrating special occasions or enjoying with a cup of coffee or tea. They melt in your mouth with their buttery goodness and are sure to be a hit with everyone!

Camotes Enmielados (Candied Sweet Potatoes)

Ingredients:

- 4 medium sweet potatoes (about 2 lbs), peeled and cut into thick slices or chunks
- 1 cone of piloncillo (about 8 oz), or substitute with dark brown sugar
- 1 cinnamon stick
- 2 cups water
- 1/2 teaspoon ground cinnamon

- 1/4 teaspoon ground cloves
- Pinch of salt
- Optional toppings: chopped nuts (like pecans or almonds), whipped cream, or vanilla ice cream

Instructions:

1. **Prepare the sweet potatoes:**
   - Peel the sweet potatoes and cut them into thick slices or large chunks. Rinse them under cold water to remove excess starch.
2. **Make the syrup:**
   - In a large pot or saucepan, combine the piloncillo (or dark brown sugar), cinnamon stick, ground cinnamon, ground cloves, salt, and water. Bring to a boil over medium-high heat, stirring occasionally to dissolve the piloncillo.
3. **Cook the sweet potatoes:**
   - Once the syrup is boiling and the piloncillo is completely dissolved, add the sweet potato slices/chunks to the pot. Reduce the heat to medium-low and simmer gently.
   - Cook the sweet potatoes in the syrup, stirring occasionally, until they are tender and the syrup has thickened slightly. This will take about 30-40 minutes, depending on the size of your sweet potato pieces. Pierce them with a fork to check for doneness.
4. **Serve:**
   - Once the sweet potatoes are tender and the syrup has thickened to your liking, remove the pot from the heat.
   - Serve the Camotes Enmielados warm or at room temperature. You can spoon some of the syrup over the sweet potatoes when serving.
5. **Optional toppings:**
   - Garnish with chopped nuts, if desired, for added texture and flavor.
   - Camotes Enmielados are traditionally served as is or with a dollop of whipped cream or a scoop of vanilla ice cream on top.

Tips:

- **Piloncillo substitute:** If you can't find piloncillo, you can use dark brown sugar as a substitute. It will still give you a rich caramel flavor.
- **Storage:** Store any leftovers of Camotes Enmielados in an airtight container in the refrigerator. They can be reheated gently on the stovetop or in the microwave before serving.
- **Variations:** Some recipes include adding a splash of orange juice or zest to the syrup for a citrusy twist. Feel free to experiment with different spices like star anise or nutmeg for added complexity.

Enjoy making and savoring this traditional Mexican dessert of Camotes Enmielados, perfect for sharing with family and friends!

Tacos de Canasta

Ingredients:

For the tacos:

- 12-15 small corn tortillas
- 2 cups refried beans (frijoles refritos), warmed
- 2 cups shredded chicken (pollo deshebrado) or beef (carne deshebrada), warmed

- 2 cups potatoes with chorizo (papas con chorizo), cooked and warmed
- 2 cups tinga de pollo (shredded chicken in chipotle sauce), warmed
- 2 cups chicharrón prensado (pressed pork cracklings in green salsa), warmed
- Optional fillings: guacamole, salsa, chopped onions, cilantro, lime wedges

For assembling:

- Vegetable oil or lard, for frying tortillas
- Large basket lined with a clean kitchen towel or parchment paper

Instructions:

1. **Prepare the fillings:**
   - Prepare your choice of fillings. You can use refried beans, shredded chicken or beef, potatoes with chorizo, tinga de pollo (chicken in chipotle sauce), chicharrón prensado (pressed pork cracklings in green salsa), or any other savory filling of your choice. Ensure they are warmed before assembling the tacos.
2. **Warm the tortillas:**
   - Heat a small amount of vegetable oil or lard in a skillet over medium heat. Briefly fry each tortilla for about 5-10 seconds on each side until softened and pliable. Drain excess oil on paper towels.
3. **Assemble the tacos:**
   - Place a spoonful of your chosen filling in the center of each tortilla. Fold the tortilla in half to form a taco shape.
4. **Stack the tacos:**
   - Assemble the filled tacos in layers inside a large basket lined with a clean kitchen towel or parchment paper. Start with a layer of tacos, then place another clean towel on top, and continue stacking the tacos in layers.
5. **Steam the tacos:**
   - Cover the basket with a lid or another towel to trap steam. Allow the tacos to steam for at least 30 minutes. This steaming process allows the flavors to meld together and the tortillas to soften further.
6. **Serve:**
   - Remove the lid or towel from the basket. Serve Tacos de Canasta warm directly from the basket.
7. **Optional toppings:**
   - Serve with optional toppings such as guacamole, salsa, chopped onions, cilantro, and lime wedges on the side. Each person can customize their tacos according to their preferences.

Tips:

- **Variations:** Feel free to experiment with different fillings based on your taste preferences. Tacos de Canasta are versatile and can accommodate various savory fillings.

- **Keep warm:** If you're not serving the tacos immediately after steaming, keep them covered in the basket to retain warmth.
- **Make ahead:** You can prepare the fillings ahead of time and warm them before assembling the tacos. This makes it easier to assemble and steam the tacos just before serving.

Enjoy making and savoring Tacos de Canasta, a delicious and authentic Mexican street food experience at home!

Sopa Azteca

Ingredients:

For the soup:

- 4 medium tomatoes, halved
- 1 onion, peeled and quartered

- 2 cloves garlic, peeled
- 1-2 dried pasilla or ancho chilies, seeded and deveined
- 1 tablespoon vegetable oil
- 6 cups chicken broth
- 1 teaspoon ground cumin
- 1 teaspoon dried oregano
- Salt and pepper, to taste
- 1 cup cooked shredded chicken breast
- 1 cup corn kernels (fresh or frozen)
- 1 lime, juiced

For serving:

- 6 corn tortillas, cut into thin strips
- Vegetable oil, for frying tortilla strips
- 1 avocado, diced
- 1/2 cup crumbled queso fresco or shredded Monterey Jack cheese
- Fresh cilantro leaves, chopped
- Lime wedges

Instructions:

1. **Prepare the soup base:**
    - Preheat your broiler. Place the halved tomatoes, quartered onion, garlic cloves, and dried chilies on a baking sheet lined with aluminum foil.
    - Drizzle with vegetable oil and season with salt and pepper. Broil for about 10 minutes, turning halfway through, until the vegetables are charred and softened.
    - Remove from the oven and let cool slightly. Remove the stems from the dried chilies.
2. **Blend the soup base:**
    - In a blender, combine the broiled tomatoes, onion, garlic, and dried chilies. Add a cup of chicken broth and blend until smooth. You may need to work in batches depending on the size of your blender.
3. **Cook the soup:**
    - Heat a large pot over medium heat. Pour the blended mixture into the pot through a fine-mesh sieve to strain out any solids.
    - Add the remaining chicken broth, ground cumin, dried oregano, and season with salt and pepper to taste. Bring the soup to a boil, then reduce the heat and let it simmer for about 15-20 minutes to allow the flavors to meld together.
4. **Prepare the tortilla strips:**
    - While the soup is simmering, heat vegetable oil in a skillet over medium-high heat. Fry the tortilla strips in batches until golden and crispy. Transfer to a paper towel-lined plate to drain excess oil. Season lightly with salt while still warm.
5. **Assemble the soup:**

- Add the shredded chicken and corn kernels to the simmering soup. Cook for an additional 5 minutes until the chicken and corn are heated through.
- Stir in the lime juice and adjust seasoning if needed.
6. **Serve:**
    - Ladle the Sopa Azteca into bowls. Top each serving with diced avocado, crispy tortilla strips, crumbled queso fresco or shredded cheese, and chopped cilantro.
    - Serve immediately with lime wedges on the side for squeezing over the soup.

Tips:

- **Variations:** You can add other toppings such as sour cream, diced tomatoes, sliced jalapeños, or a drizzle of Mexican crema for added richness.
- **Make it vegetarian:** Substitute vegetable broth for chicken broth and omit the shredded chicken. You can also add more vegetables like zucchini or bell peppers.
- **Storage:** Sopa Azteca is best served fresh. Store leftover soup and toppings separately in airtight containers in the refrigerator for up to 2-3 days. Reheat gently on the stove before serving.

Enjoy making and savoring this delicious and hearty Sopa Azteca, perfect for warming up on chilly days or for a comforting meal any time of the year!

Nopalitos Salad (Cactus Salad)

Ingredients:

- 3-4 nopales (cactus pads), cleaned and diced
- 1 tomato, diced
- 1/2 onion, finely chopped

- 1/2 cup chopped cilantro
- 1 jalapeño or serrano pepper, finely chopped (optional, for heat)
- 2 tablespoons olive oil
- 2 tablespoons fresh lime juice
- Salt and pepper, to taste
- Queso fresco, crumbled (optional, for garnish)
- Avocado slices (optional, for serving)

Instructions:

1. **Prepare the nopales:**
   - Start by cleaning the cactus pads (nopales). Using a sharp knife, carefully trim off the edges and any remaining thorns. Rinse them well under cold water to remove any residual sap.
   - Bring a large pot of water to a boil. Add the cleaned nopales and cook for about 8-10 minutes, or until tender. Drain and rinse with cold water to stop the cooking process. Let them cool completely.
   - Once cooled, dice the nopales into small pieces and place them in a large mixing bowl.
2. **Assemble the salad:**
   - Add the diced tomato, finely chopped onion, chopped cilantro, and chopped jalapeño or serrano pepper (if using) to the bowl with the nopales.
3. **Dress the salad:**
   - Drizzle olive oil and fresh lime juice over the salad ingredients. Season with salt and pepper to taste.
4. **Mix well:**
   - Gently toss all the ingredients together until well combined and evenly coated with the dressing.
5. **Serve:**
   - Transfer the Nopalitos Salad to a serving dish or individual plates.
6. **Garnish (optional):**
   - Sprinkle crumbled queso fresco on top for added texture and flavor.
   - Serve the salad with avocado slices on the side, if desired.

Tips:

- **Variations:** You can customize this salad by adding other ingredients such as grilled corn kernels, diced bell peppers, or black beans.
- **Preparation:** If you prefer a smokier flavor, you can grill the nopales instead of boiling them. Simply brush them with olive oil and grill over medium-high heat until tender and slightly charred.
- **Storage:** Nopalitos Salad can be stored in an airtight container in the refrigerator for up to 2-3 days. The flavors often meld together more after sitting overnight.

Enjoy this vibrant and flavorful Nopalitos Salad as a side dish or a light main course, perfect for celebrating the freshness of Mexican flavors!

Rosca de Reyes

Ingredients:

For the dough:

- 4 cups all-purpose flour

- 1/2 cup granulated sugar
- 1/2 cup unsalted butter, softened
- 3/4 cup warm milk
- 2 1/4 teaspoons active dry yeast (1 packet)
- 3 eggs
- 1 teaspoon vanilla extract
- Zest of 1 orange
- Zest of 1 lemon
- 1/2 teaspoon salt

For the decoration:

- 1 egg, beaten (for egg wash)
- Candied fruits (figs, cherries, orange peel) or chopped nuts (optional)
- Confectioners' sugar, for dusting

For the filling (optional):

- 1/2 cup chopped nuts (almonds, pecans, or walnuts)
- 1/2 cup packed brown sugar
- 1 teaspoon ground cinnamon
- 2 tablespoons unsalted butter, melted

Instructions:

1. **Activate the yeast:**
   - In a small bowl, dissolve 1 tablespoon of sugar in the warm milk. Sprinkle the yeast over the milk and let it sit for about 5-10 minutes until foamy.
2. **Make the dough:**
   - In a large mixing bowl or the bowl of a stand mixer fitted with a dough hook, combine the softened butter, remaining sugar, eggs, vanilla extract, orange zest, lemon zest, and salt. Mix until well combined.
   - Add half of the flour and the yeast mixture to the bowl. Mix until incorporated. Gradually add the remaining flour, mixing until a soft dough forms.
   - Knead the dough on a floured surface or continue with the stand mixer for about 8-10 minutes until the dough is smooth and elastic. If the dough is too sticky, add a little more flour, a tablespoon at a time.
3. **First rise:**
   - Place the dough in a greased bowl, cover with a clean kitchen towel or plastic wrap, and let it rise in a warm place for about 1-2 hours until doubled in size.
4. **Prepare the filling (optional):**
   - While the dough is rising, prepare the filling if using. Combine chopped nuts, brown sugar, cinnamon, and melted butter in a small bowl. Mix until well combined.
5. **Shape the Rosca:**

- Once the dough has risen, punch it down to deflate it. Divide the dough into two equal portions. Shape each portion into a long rope and twist them together to form a ring or oval shape. Pinch the ends together to seal.
- Place the shaped dough on a parchment-lined baking sheet. Cover loosely with plastic wrap and let it rise again in a warm place for about 1 hour until puffed.

6. **Preheat the oven:**
   - Preheat your oven to 350°F (175°C) during the last 15-20 minutes of the second rise.
7. **Decorate and bake:**
   - Brush the top of the Rosca de Reyes with beaten egg to give it a shiny finish. Decorate with candied fruits or chopped nuts, pressing them lightly into the dough.
   - Bake in the preheated oven for 25-30 minutes, or until the Rosca is golden brown and sounds hollow when tapped on the bottom.
8. **Finish and serve:**
   - Remove the Rosca de Reyes from the oven and let it cool on a wire rack.
   - Once cooled, dust the Rosca generously with confectioners' sugar.
   - Optional: Insert a small figurine of baby Jesus (or a dried bean) into the underside of the Rosca for the tradition of finding the surprise.
9. **Serve and enjoy:**
   - Slice and serve the Rosca de Reyes with hot chocolate or atole on Día de Reyes (Three Kings' Day) or any festive occasion.

Tips:

- **Variations:** Some recipes include a filling of chopped nuts and brown sugar, which can be sprinkled over the dough before shaping the Rosca.
- **Decoration:** Get creative with the candied fruits or nuts you use to decorate the Rosca. Traditional colors include red, green, and yellow for a festive look.
- **Storage:** Rosca de Reyes is best enjoyed fresh on the day it's made. Store any leftovers in an airtight container at room temperature for up to 2 days, though it may become slightly dry.

Enjoy making this festive and delicious Rosca de Reyes, a wonderful tradition to celebrate with family and friends!

www.ingramcontent.com/pod-product-compliance
Lightning Source LLC
LaVergne TN
LVHW081605060526
838201LV00054B/2084